BEING, EVOLUTION, AND IMMORTALITY

Dr. Pitirim A. Sorokin of Harvard University has called this work "an outstanding contribution, not only to the philosophy of Sri Aurobindo, but to the philosophical problems discussed in it."

Dr. Frederic Spiegelberg of Stanford University, in his Foreword, comments on the gratification of seeing "a thinker at work who is truly both a devoted follower of a great master and an independent thinker of the widest scope of erudition."

The author himself, in his Preface, sets the tone of his work in the words: "It is by responding to the periodic challenge of history that man can keep advancing on the road of evolution." This book is a superb response to the challenge of this critical moment in the history of humankind.

The need in every age to reinterpret and reintegrate the cumulative knowledge resulting from man's unconquerable intellect with the undying spiritual realities which underlie and complement that knowledge is here met with a new and refreshing synthesis. Dr. Chaudhuri's wide range of understanding encompasses many complementary and mutually enriching aspects of our evolutionary advance. The thoughtful reader cannot fail to reach new insights.

Portions of this book were originally published as *The Philosophy of Integralism*. The text has been updated, some of it rewritten, and new material has been added, in keeping with the author's conviction that ancient truths must ever find expression in ways that meet the need of the times.

Dr. Chaudhuri, who came to the United States in 1951 at the invitation of Dr. Spiegelberg, is Professor of Philosophy, President of the California Institute of Asian Studies, San Francisco, and President of the Cultural Integration Fellowship. He is the author of the Quest best seller, *Integral Yoga*.

BEING, EVOLUTION, AND IMMORTALITY
An Outline of Integral Philosophy

by

HARIDAS CHAUDHURI

Professor of Integral Philosophy,
and President, California Institute
of Asian Studies, San Francisco

Foreword by

FREDERIC SPIEGELBERG

Professor of Asiatic and Slavic Studies
Stanford University, Northern California

A QUEST BOOK

Published under a grant from the Kern Foundation

THE THEOSOPHICAL PUBLISHING HOUSE
Wheaton, Ill. U.S.A.
Madras, India / London, England

© Haridas Chaudhuri, 1974
First Quest Edition published by the Theosophical Publishing House, Wheaton, Illinois, a department of The Theosophical Society in America, 1974

Chaudhuri, Haridas.
  Being, evolution, and immortality.

  (A Quest book)
  Second ed. published in 1967 under title: The philosophy of integralism.
  Includes bibliographical references.
  1. Ghose, Aurobindo, 1872-1950. I. Title.
B5134.G42C35   1974   181'.4   74-4821
ISBN 0-8356-0449-7

PRINTED IN THE UNITED STATES OF AMERICA

TO
SRI AUROBINDO

Who brought into the author's life
A new rhythm and a new light

FOREWORD

Srī Krsna says in the Gītā (17, 2f) that man's devotion is of three kinds; it is characterised by sattva, rajas, and tamas. That is, the quality given to one's devotion depends on one's particular psychological nature, which may be bright and intelligent, fierce and moody, or dull and lethargic. In Sri Aurobindo's translation: "The faith of each man takes the shape given to it by his stuff of being."

What is true for *śradhā*, faith, is equally true for the attitude of a man to his guru. Observing the history of religions through the ages, we find that after the great periods of revelation by a powerful teacher, usually an immediate downfall sets in, because disciples of the prophet, the starters and organizers of a new movement, are often determined by the characteristics of rajas or tamas, either fiercely fighting in an unreasonable and intolerant way, or destroying the quality of their message by prejudices and stubbornness. Destructive crusades on the one hand and over-organization that leads to stagnation on the other hand have been the determining factors of religious decadence throughout all history.

Just as this is true for all past periods, so can we equally observe the same process today in many new movements; few great visions of mankind have escaped the fate of becoming a cult. This has happened and is happening today in East and in West. Westerners observing developments in India are in addition to that often worried about the time-honored trend of guru-worship which, in spite of its tremendous advantages, carries in it also the danger of blind allegiance, in which the master's ideas are preserved, to be sure, but, as it were, in frozen form, and without the expanding possibilities, without the exploding, dynamic element which they carried while still connected with a live prophetic vision.

Apostolic succession has this double character of preservation and petrifaction. For an illustration, let us take the example of the artistic tradition. To live up to the high standards of the masters of classical periods has all too often been misinterpreted as having the meaning of copying them slavishly. Such imitation, perfect as it may seemingly be, lacks the most decisive element of the master's own style, i.e., his creativity, and is therefore not an "imitation" at all.

The great creative masters of India's philosophic renaissance have shared this same fate. The refreshing greatness of Vivekananda consisted primarily in the fact that he was not slavishly following his great master, Sri Ramakrishna at all. In the same way it is most gratifying to see in Haridas Chaudhuri a thinker at work who is truly both a devoted follower of a great master and an independent thinker of the widest possible scope of erudition. Chaudhuri's authenticity as a foremost interpreter of Sri Aurobindo's all-pervading system is guaranteed by the master's own approval of Chaudhuri's coming to San Francisco, where, as Professor, he has been serving as the most reliable teacher of this culmination of India's spirituality.

On the other hand, Chaudhuri's creative thinking and systematic combining ability has become obvious to all who have come into the sphere of his winning personality and who have heard his lectures and contributions to the regular colloquium-sessions, where the members of the faculty were wrestling with each other in the most radical search for truth and for its expression in human thought, with fierce concentration on this highest goal alone, withholding necessarily at the same time all regard for personal and all-too-personal feelings and weaknesses of the participants. To join with Chaudhuri in this "ruthless" process of the colloquium has proved to all those participating to be an acid bath of the mind, cleaning unrelentingly all prejudices and cherished half-truths away.

The reading of this book will have the same effect on the reader. Chaudhuri happily combines the technique of a complete perusal of all possible theories on the subject on the basis of his profound erudition in philosophy East and West with the light-giving solution that he has found in treading the path opened by his sublime guru's vision.

FREDERIC SPIEGELBERG

AUTHOR'S PREFACE

The imperative of every new age is a newly integrated world-view, a new synthesis of past wisdom and future aspirations and ideals. It is by responding to the periodic challenge of history that man can keep advancing on the road of evolution. And this response can become a creative advance only by bringing together in a comprehensive *Weltanschauung* the latest findings in our knowledge of *fact and existence* on the one hand and freshly-won insights in the realm of *essence and value* on the other.

In other words, the essential need of our present age is a creative synthesis of the East's spiritual wisdom and the West's scientific knowledge, the East's insight into the mystery of Being and the West's discovery of the miracle of Evolution, the East's revelation of the imperishable spiritual values and the West's refinement of the technology, not only mechanical but also conceptual and organizational technology, necessary for materialization on earth of truth, love, and peace.

In my book *Integral Yoga,* I indicated how the material and spiritual values of life, existential and ontological values, social, economic and political values on the one hand and psychological, religious and mystical values on the other can be harmonized in an unfolding symphony of creative living.

The present work — *Being, Evolution, and Immortality* — is a companion volume to *Integral Yoga*. It sketches a brief outline of the basic concepts of Integral Nondualism which constitute the theoretical foundation of Integral Yoga as the art of integrated living. It may also be designated as integral Vedanta or Integral Humanism.

From the integral perspective, Being, the ground of the universe, is integral fullness or plenum (pūrṇam), the wholeness of all life and existence. It is the kind of fullness which remains ever full, no matter how much is taken away from it (p. 10). Western thought in the main has a tendency to equate Being with the space-time continuum, with evolution and history, with the cosmic process. It is inclined to ignore the nontemporal depth dimension of both nature and man, the inexhaustible ground and encompassing medium of all existence. Alienated from the depth dimension, man loses his sense of higher values, allows his indwelling hidden springs of love and compassion to dry up. Eastern spirituality on the other hand has a tendency on the whole to equate Being with the nontemporal transcendence, with the trans-historical spirit, with the immortal self. It is inclined to ignore the profound significance of space-time, of evolution and history, of man's destiny on earth.

The philosophy of integral nondualism holds together in a higher synthesis the Western vision of man's evolution on earth and the Eastern vision of man's oneness with the realm of eternal values, his immortal rootedness in the cosmic intelligence operative in nature.

The light of integral Being-cognition, what Sri Aurobindo has called the Supermind (ṛta-cit, satyam ṛtam vṛhat) provides the dynamic link between evolution and immortality, history and eternity, the space-time continuum and pure transcendence. The integral methodology which is essential for the unfoldment of the integral truth-vision combines the scientific *know-how* of the West with the spiritual *be-how* of the East. As briefly indicated in the final chapter, it harmonizes the art of integrated living (integral yoga or self discipline), with the systems view characteristic of contemporary scientific thinking.

Be it noted that the present volume is no more than a very sketchy outline of the integral world-view presented as much as possible in nonmetaphysical and nondichotomous terms. In reconciling the highest cultural values of East and West, it also achieves a dynamic synthesis of science and religion, logic and mysticism, existentialism and essentialism, evolutionism and transcendentalism. It is hoped that competent philosophers dedicated to East-West integration will come forward to develop further the value-synthesis set forth herein. There is no doubt in my mind that such an integration alone can lay the foundation for one unified international family of man.

I wish to take this opportunity of offering my sincere thanks to The Theosophical Publishing House for its promptness and care in presenting this book to the American public. Many thanks are also due to Prithwi Singh Nahar of Sri Aurobindo Ashram, Pondicherry, for his kind permission to use all material needed for this publication. Among others to whom I feel indebted for their valuable suggestions and friendly encouragement are Dr. Frederic Spiegelberg of Stanford University; Dr. Robert McDermott of Baruch College, New York; Dr. Karan Singh, Cabinet Minister, the Government of India, New Delhi; Sri Surendra Mohan Ghose, former President, Bengal National Congress, Calcutta; Bina Chaudhuri, my wife and secretary, whose patience and understanding have proved inexhaustible; Barbara Wilson, our student and friend, and Dr. Enoch Haga, Academic Vice-President, California Institute of Asian Studies, San Francisco. Finally, it should be noted that Chapter 17 on The Supermind was first published in the special Sri Aurobindo Centenary issue of the International Philosophical Quarterly (New York: Fordham University Press, June 1972). My grateful thanks are due to the Editor for his kind permission to incorporate that article in this volume.

San Francisco   Haridas Chaudhuri
February 1974.

CONTENTS

Chapter 1

THE INTEGRAL APPROACH OF SRI AUROBINDO

Sri Aurobindo ranks among the world's foremost mystic seers, poets and philosophers. As a spiritual leader he is amazingly dynamic. As a speculative thinker he is profoundly creative. He has given to the world a very comprehensive philosophical system, a new spiritual synthesis, an inspiring *Weltanschauung*. But what is more important, he has also given to the world a complete art of integral living. It points the way to dynamic integration of the material and spiritual values of life. It is a call to the reconstruction of human life and society on the basis of abiding spiritual values. The basic principles of integral living are outlined in Sri Aurobindo's "The Synthesis of Yoga." The central concepts of the integral world-view are elucidated in his *magnum opus* "The Life Divine."

The philosophical synthesis inherent in the teaching of Sri Aurobindo may variously be described as Integral Vedānta, Integral Nondualism, or just Integralism. The implications of the above designations are briefly stated in the following paragraphs.

The philosophical outlook of Sri Aurobindo may be designated Integral Vedānta insofar as it is the reaffirmation of the original teaching of the Vedas, the Upaniṣads, and the Bhagavadgītā in all the richness of their spiritual insight. His commentaries on these ancient scriptures present the timeless truth in a form especially appropriate to the present times.

The Integral Interpretation of Vedánta

Broadly speaking, there are three principal modes of interpretation of Vedānta: unqualified nondualism (kevala-advaita), qualified nondualism (viśiṣṭa-advaita), and dualism (dvaita). Unqualified nondualism lays stress upon the concept of Being as formless and indeterminable (Nirguṇa Brahman). So much so that the unique individual and the creative universal (Jīva and Īśwara), even though they are not considered nonexistent, are declared unreal from the standpoint of ultimate reality. The practical bearing of this way of thinking is a greater or lesser degree of world-negating and life-denying ascetic tendency. Monastic life represents the spiritual path par excellence.

Qualified nondualism in its various forms lays stress upon the concept of Being as the all-embracing personal God (Saguṇa Brahman), endowed with supernatural qualities and powers. Impersonality is explained as the all-pervasive radiance of the Divine Person. Formlessness is explained as the immeasurable richness of form, just as the priceless means immeasurable price. The unqualified is explained as that which is void of impure natural qualities, but endowed with excellent supernatural qualities without number. The practical bearing of this way of thinking is a religious-emotional way of living oriented to the supernatural. Under its influence a person easily abandons himself to religious rapture and ecstasy, somewhat unmindful of the need for social participation on the one hand and the serenity of wisdom on the other.

Dualism lays stress upon the concept of Being as an external transcendent Deity ruling the multitude of finite spirits. Individual selves are existentially separate not only from each other, but also from the sovereign God. The consequence of this way of thinking is an accentuation of the individual's feeling of sinfulness and his absolute dependence upon an external Power. Dualism compromises the unity, infinity and all-comprehending character of the Divine. It militates against the mystic realization of the individual's intrinsic freedom and essential oneness of being with the Supreme.

Sri Aurobindo maintains that according to the original teaching of the Vedas, the Upaniṣads, and the Gītā, impersonal Being, personal God, and individual self, are three inseparable and equally real modes of existence of the same supreme reality. They are all essential factors in the structure of Being. Impersonality signifies the formless and boundless essence of Being. Personal God represents the power of creative intelligence inherent in Being. The individual self represents Being in its individualized mode of existence. Each individual self represents a distinct and unique value. It reflects the joy of self-differentiation of the cosmic energy. The cosmic energy is personal in the sense that it has a deep interest in creating and preserving the unique values of individuality. It is only by a one-sided and exaggerated emphasis upon either the individual or the universal or the transcendent that the traditional schools of Vedānta get entrenched in their opposition to each other.

Harmonization of Experience

Integral Vedānta is integral nondualism. Or, it may just be called integralism. Integralism is a comprehensive and connected view of the nature of the universe on the basis of an integration of all the cognitive resources of human personality. Most of the conflicting philosophical systems in the West lay exaggerated emphasis upon this or that particular area of human experience. For instance, materialism is usually the philosophical outlook of a physicist or natural scientist, whereas spiritualism is a religious man's philosophy of life. Vitalism is usually the philosophy of a biologist turned philosopher; whereas a moralist usually builds his philosophy along the lines of ethical idealism or idealistic evolutionism. Pragmatism is usually the philosophy of a man of action; whereas absolute idealism is the *Weltanschauung* of a speculative thinker of retiring disposition. Integral philosophy holds that in order to develop a synoptic vision of reality a coordination of the different areas of human experience is imperatively necessary. Such a coordination is in its turn possible only on the basis of a perfect integration of the different aspects of human personality. An integral view of reality can grow only out of an integration of one's total being.

An integral vision of reality implies two things. First, it implies immediate contact with ultimate reality in its manifold richness of content. Secondly, it implies a breadth of vision, a comprehensive outlook, reconciling such different areas of human experience as common sense, science, art, morality and religion, and also such different phases of the spirit in man as waking, dream, sleep and mystic experience.

While the practical man overstresses the reality of time, the mystic often overemphasizes the reality of the timeless. Mystic experience is sometimes carried to such an extreme that the world of plurality is condemned as an unreal appearance, void of intrinsic significance. Integral philosophy reconciles supersensuous mystic experience with sensuous world experience. According to Sri Aurobindo, the fullness of spiritual realization reaffirms the world of space and time on the unshakable foundation of the eternal. It harmonizes all fragmentary human experiences in a comprehensive truth-vision.

It is vital to the understanding of the philosophy of integralism to realize that a harmonization of experience is not possible through mere criticism of the categories of common sense and science. Nor is it possible through mere logico-empirical analysis of the different types of proposition. Nor is it, on the other hand, possible by means of rationalization of onesided mystical experience. An harmonization of experience can be achieved only by means of full self-integration i.e., integration of the intellectual, moral, emotional, and spiritual aspects of personality.

Comprehensive Synthesis

Integral philosophy embodies a very comprehensive metaphysical synthesis. It reconciles the doctrines of change and permanence. It reconciles evolutionism and eternalism. It reconciles mysticism and monadism.

Modern thought posits change as the stuff of all existence. As Bergson says, "To exist is to change, and to change is to grow and mature."[1] It may be added that to mature is to realize some new emergent value. This is in striking contrast with ancient metaphysical thinking. Ancient metaphysics lays stress upon permanence as the essence of reality. It assumes that the eternal alone is real. Being must be unchanging and unchangeable. The logical sequel to that assumption is that change is more or less unreal or illusory.

For instance, the doctrine of permanence is common to both Śankara-Vedānta and Platonic idealism. But it acquires different meanings and values in the two different systems. Śankara-Vedānta identifies the permanent as the formless and indeterminable Being. So the world of perishing things and mortal beings must be unreal. It is the product of nescience (Māyā). Even though existent from the standpoint of ignorance, it is illusory from the standpoint of the eternal.

Platonic idealism identifies the permanent as eternal essences, forms, ideas. Ideas are unchanging and unchangeable self-subsistent entities. They are the components of pure being. The world of flux and flow is torn between being and nonbeing. Ever-changing objects of the world are shadows or imitations of the ideal world of perfection. Their ontological status is vitiated by the contamination of an alien stuff, formless matter.

According to integral philosophy, change is no less real than permanence. Change and permanence represent two equally real dimensions of Being. The temporal and the

---

[1] Henry Bergson, *Creative Evolution*, Arthur Mitchell trans. (London: Macmillan & Co., 1920), p. 8.

nontemporal represent two equally real aspects of existence. Evolution and perfection are equally significant poises of being of the Supreme.

According to ancient oriental metaphysics, determinate objects are unreal names and forms (*nāma-rūpa*) of one fundamental substance. For instance, different types of gold ornament, however valuable and beautiful, are unreal modifications of their basic substance, gold. They are fashioned out of gold, and are eventually re-absorbed into gold. According to Platonic idealism, the aesthetic forms or designs embodied in different types of gold ornament are the basic reality. Particular gold ornaments are only images or imitations of immutable designs. The recalcitrant stuff of gold somewhat compromises the perfection of those designs. They also undergo wear and tear and have eventually to be melted back into gold. So they are unreal.

The integral viewpoint holds that particular things are no less real than the universal substance of which they are made. A beautiful piece of gold ornament is no less real than the substance of gold on the one hand and the aesthetic design on the other. In fact, it partakes of the reality of both. Both matter and form receive their fulfillment in it. It represents a unique emergent value. It is the meeting-point of two dimensions of permanence. On the one hand, it is a determinate mode of expression of gold. On the other, it is the actualization of a beautiful design or idea. Without particular determination, gold has little use or value. Without definite actualization, design is lifeless abstraction.

Similarly, the little rose that blossoms in the garden is no less real than the elements of earth, water, light, etc. of which it is made. Nor is it less real than the idea of roseness. Both matter and form combine here to give rise to a very precious and unique emergent value, which is supremely real, however transient.

Similarly again, an individual human being whose individuality has blossomed to the full is no less real than the universal life-force or the eternal pattern of humanity which it embodies. In truth, the highly evolved individual carries reality to a new height. He hits a new depth of existence. He is the meeting-point of time and eternity. On the one hand, he is a unique mode of expression of formless Being (Brahman). On the other, he is the incarnation of an eternal value, an imperishable idea. Formless Being and bodiless Form combine to make him doubly real and supremely valuable. He adds to permanence the new dimension of actuality. He actualizes a unique potential of the creative urge of Being.

In order to appreciate fully the significance of the integral view of reality as the unity of change and permanence, it is necessary to shake loose from the old obsessional metaphysics of permanence. It is necessary to revise some of our old rigid habits of thinking. It is necessary to grasp the meaning and reality of change and evolution, of growth and progress, without discarding the ancient sages' view of the eternal as the stable foundation of all change.

The Value of Individuality

It should be evident from the above that individuality is an intrinsic value, an essential component of reality. It is a significant mode of expression of Being. In its inmost essence, it is the product, not of ignorance, but of the superconscient creative urge of Being. It is an active center of dynamic self-expression of the Supreme. In that case, true wisdom cannot consist in mere self-negation in an absolute void, or in self-annihilation in the formless absolute. The path of wisdom rather lies in the realization of one's essential oneness with the whole of existence and in the reconstruction of one's life on the basis of that realization.

Since the individual is essentially an active and unique center of the universal life-force, the highest goal of human life cannot consist in withdrawal from life and social action. It cannot consist in mere emancipation from the cycle of birth and death. Or in mere liberation from the dualities of joy and sorrow, knowledge and ignorance. It must assume the form of dynamic self-identification with the creative purpose of life, with the forward march of the evolutionary world-spirit.

Since inherent in Being is an evolutionary urge, a creative impulse, the *summum bonum* of life cannot consist in mere static contemplation of eternal verities or in mystic flight into transcendental ecstasies. The full fruition of life lies in active participation in the boundless joy of creation.

Finally, since the human individual, by virtue of his self-consciousness, is capable of discovering the element of pure transcendence and freedom in life, he is most creative when he is free. On the attainment of spiritual liberation, he may freely choose either to remain in static transcendental peace, or to participate in the creative flow of life. The latter alternative is no doubt a fuller ideal of life, because it implies a fuller experience of Being as the unity of transcendence and creativity. It implies a complete integration of human personality, harmonizing its introverted and extroverted tendencies.

Foundation of Integral Yoga

The philosophy of integralism is the foundation of integral yoga. It is the theoretical basis of the art of harmonious and creative living. The secret of integral yoga lies in integrated living, true to the kindred points of time and eternity. Inwardly, it is union with the eternal. Outwardly, it is dedication to the cosmic purpose of evolution. Inwardly, it is blissful self-realization. Outwardly, it is creative self-expression out of inner illumination. On the one hand, it is self-transcendence in the vastness of the infinite. On the other, it is self-transformation as a fit vehicle of the infinite. It is complete self-fulfillment in terms of wisdom, love and selfless action, harmoniously blended together.

Integral philosophy embodies an insight into the fullness of Being. To know Being steady and whole is to grasp the reality of evolution as the creative self-expression of the eternal. Evolution and timeless perfection are inseparable aspects of Being. So when a person attains full wisdom, he cannot remain passive, aloof and withdrawn from life, turning a deaf ear to the cries of human anguish. Compassion spontaneously flows from the right kind of wisdom. And compassion knows no rest until it issues forth into the right kind of action. It sets forth the ideal of constructive refashioning of life and society into a growing image of the divine.

Chapter 2

THE INTEGRAL WORLD-VIEW

Integral philosophy aims to comprehend Being in its multi-dimensional fullness. It carries to fruition the concept of fullness in the Upaniṣads. It has been stated in the Īśa Upaniṣads:[1]

> That is full; this is full.
> The full comes out of the full.
> Taking the full from the full
> The full itself remains.

This is an affirmation of the supreme truth that God and the world, the infinite and the finite, the universal and the individual, are inseparable aspects of the same Being. The Upaniṣads declare that Being is on the one hand indeterminable (nirguṇa), and on the other the creative source of all determinations (saguṇa). The indeterminable silence and the creative eloquence are two equally real dimensions of ultimate reality. Neither of them should be reduced to an unreal appearance, or to a subordinate feature of the other.

Even nonbeing is an essential element in the structure of total Being. An adequate grasp of this profound truth can lay the foundation for reconciliation of Hinduism and Buddhism which have fought with each other for centuries in the history of Indian thought.

Buddhism affirms that Nonbeing, the absolute void or emptiness (śūnyatā) is the key concept of spiritual philosophy. All existing things emerge into being out of the

---

[1] Radhakrishnan, *The Principal Upaniṣads* (New York: Humanities Press, Inc., 1969). p. 566.

creative vastness of Nonbeing. They run their course of transient existence like passing clouds, or rolling waves, or lightning flashes, and then vanish into nothingness again. But this Nonbeing is, for Buddha, not a mere abstraction of thought. Nor is it a nihilistic concept, a powerless zero. Nonbeing is for him the substance of supreme spiritual enlightenment. It is the most fundamental experiential fact. It is endowed with infinite creativity. That is why the Buddha's message of the creative void ushered into existence the golden age of Indian history. It brought about a new all-around cultural efflorescence characterized by boundless creativity in art, philosophy, religion, social service, and humanitarian work, in trade and commerce and even in political empire building upon the basis of universal compassion. It produced the greatest empire of ancient India. It produced in Aśoka, the great saint-emperor, one of the greatest emperors of the world. It established itself as the beacon light of spiritual unfoldment to the whole continent of Asia, nay, to the whole civilized world known at the time.

Śankara Vedānta repudiated Buddhism mainly for its heretical tendency. Followers of the Buddha, much contrary to the master's distaste for new sects and metaphysical systems, became increasingly engaged in founding new metaphysical schools and religious orders. They went beyond the master's avowed mission of restoring the ancient way, that is, the original teaching of the Upaniṣads by clearing away the roadblocks of ritualism, intellectualism, and extreme asceticism. In other words, followers of the Buddha were trying to establish Buddhism as a separate religion, denying the authority of the Vedas and Upaniṣads. As a result of this divisive tendency the continuity of Hindu culture was in danger of being disrupted. So the great philosopher Śankara wanted to stop this. He laid stress upon the positive aspects of the concept of Being. He interpreted the pure essence of Being in terms of formless existence, undifferentiated consciousness, and spontaneous delight.

Śankara sought to preserve the continuity of Indian culture stemming from the Vedas and the Upaniṣads. He fought with all his might to eliminate heretical and disruptive forces. He made concessions to popular imagination in the interests of peace and order in society. He made compromises with the upholders of the social status quo in the interest of peaceful evolution. He regarded even personal God as a manifestation of Being, viewed from the standpoint of the world. He had no difficulty in providing a philosophical basis even for the many gods of popular imagination. They are real from the standpoint of ignorance, answering to the emotional needs of ordinary people. They vanish as unreal on the attainment of spiritual enlightenment. Thus Śankara tried to bridge the gulf between philosophy and religion, between mystic vision and popular imagination.

Buddha's emphasis upon Nonbeing as the negation of all anthropomorphic notions of God and of wishful thoughts about human destiny, was consistent with his historic mission as an uncompromising social and religious reformer. In a later period of time, Śankara's positive formulation of Being in the light of the highest terms of human experience became historically necessary. Śankara was concerned with the preservation of the continuity of Indian culture and the spiritual cohesion of Hindu society.

Now, from the spiritual standpoint, Buddha's creative Nonbeing and Śankara's formless Being are identical. They are two aspects, negative and positive aspects, of the same ontological Fullness (Pūrṇam). Being which is void of any particular feature or attribute is indistinguishable from Nonbeing. Both creative nonbeing and indeterminable Being represent reality in its pure supracosmic transcendence. Pure transcendence is indeed the profoundest depth of man's spiritual insight.

Hegel made a very profound statement when he said that pure Being is identical with Nonbeing. But unfortunately, for Hegel, both Being and Nonbeing were mere abstractions of thought. They were only conceptual generalities. That is only to be expected. Hegel's approach to reality was detached, all too logical, and abstractly speculative. He had no existential concern in truth. He had only a theoretical interest in the objective image of truth. Consequently he had no experiential contact with the timeless essence of Being. It was beyond his depth to comprehend the full existential and ontological significance of Being as identical with Nonbeing.

An integral insight into the oneness of Being and Nonbeing in pure transcendence provides the basis upon which to reconcile Buddhism and Hinduism. In the Upaniṣads we find that sometimes it is stated that Nonbeing was at the beginning, all existing things came out of Nonbeing.[2] Sometimes again it is stated that at the beginning was Being, all existing things came out of Being.[3] Properly understood, there is no contradiction here, because Being which is the source of all things is no-thing in particular. It is no-being, no determinate mode of existence. In the ultimate ontological reference, Being and Nonbeing are indeed identical.

But the experience of supracosmic transcendence is also only a phase of spiritual growth, not its ultimate goal. Just as an ordinary person is blindly attached to the world, an ascetic mystic or contemplative can be blinded by the dazzling light of transcendence. He may be so dazzled as to ignore the reality and significance of the world process. Whereas the man in bondage is blind to the transcendental grandeur of the spirit, the mystic may become blind to the creative glory of life.

Theistic Schools of Vedānta

Exclusive emphasis upon the transcendental aspect of Being tends to produce a negative attitude to life and the world. This is not necessary, but this is a fact of history. Such an exclusive emphasis is a reaction against the aver-

---

[2] *Taittirīya Upaniṣad* II. 7. 1.
[3] *Chāndogya Upaniṣad* VI. 2. 1.

age man's blind attachment to the vanities of life and to
the transient things of the world. It is a necessary phase
of man's search for spiritual values. But it is only a phase
of spiritual growth, not its ultimate goal. From attachment to material goods one may swing at the opposite
extreme into an attachment to an ascetic denial of the
material. Out of the frying pan of transience one may
fall into the fire of all-negating transcendence. And that
is exactly what happened with medieval asceticism, supernaturalism, otherworldliness and transcendentalism. It
happened in all those countries, Eastern and Western,
which were seriously searching for the highest spiritual
truth. The monastic order became the symbol of self-
perfection. In the West supranaturalism and religious
otherworldliness were the main forms that transcendentalism assumed. In India transcendentalism was more mystical and philosophical in outlook. It received its highest
expression in Buddha and Śankara. It performed no
doubt an important function in man's quest of the spiritual truth. But in the course of time its negative feature—
its world and life negating character—began to come to
the fore. Consequently, we find that the transcendentalism of the Buddha and Śankara had to be strenuously
combated in later times by the theistic schools of Vedānta.
All such Vedānta teachers as Rāmānuja, Nimbārka, Val-
labha, Madhva and Chaitanya voiced their protest against
transcendentalism and its concomitant negativism. They
did so even at the sacrifice of full comprehension of the
value and significance of formless Being. They considered
Śankara as only a Buddha in disguise.

Theistic Vedānta teachers emphasized dynamic Being
or Personal God as the Supreme. In their view, attribute-
lessness does not signify any superior dimension or mode
of existence of Being. It is only a characteristic of the
sovereign Godhead. Being is attributeless not in the sense
that it is void of powers and attributes, but because it is
endowed with infinite attributes. It is quality-less not
because it is void of qualities but because its qualitative

richness is immeasurable. When we say that a diamond
is priceless we do not mean that it has no value but only
that its value is immeasurable. Similarly God is quality-
less in the sense that he possesses an infinite number of
such auspicious qualities as wisdom, love, mercy, benevolent power, beatitude, etc. Moreover God is free from
all negative and vicious qualities and powers. Or it may
be said that God is endowed with supernatural qualities
and powers and is untarnished by the natural qualities.

Now, as hinted above, the theistic position is a fall from
the lofty vision that Buddha and Śankara attained. It is
a fall from the height of pure nondualistic vision of the
truth and of the formless essence of Being. But it represents the historical necessity to call people's attention back
to the reality and spiritual significance of the world. The
reality of the world can be founded only on the concept of
dynamic Being. The spiritual significance of the world
can be based only upon the concept of some kind of divine
creator. And the intrinsic value of life, especially of
human personality, can be based only upon the concept
of a divine ruler of the universe, personally interested in
the growth and preservation of finite spirits.

The concept of a personal God is necessary to sustain a
significant scheme of spiritual values in life. God is a
just and merciful ruler of the world. He is the loving
world-spirit guiding the destinies of man. He stands for
such supreme values as truth, justice, love, mercy, etc.
He represents a disapproval of greed and violence, injustice and barbarism, cruelty and wickedness. He sets a
definite standard for ethical conduct. He provides the
metaphysical and religious foundation for the conception
of duty. He also fulfills man's emotional need for love
and devotion, for prayer and worship. He answers to
man's longing for security and affectionate dependability.

So theistic schools of Vedānta began to flourish in later
Hinduism. Their influence permeated the masses of the
people. All manner of anthropomorphic conceptions of
personal God began to appear. And such anthropomorphic

conceptions began also to be taken often literally, giving rise to idolatrous tendencies in religious practice.

The theistic schools of Vedānta were joined by the theistic schools of Tantra. Tantra contributed to the spiritual heritage of India a very bold affirmative note. It not only emphasized the positive spiritual attributes of God as the creative world-spirit (Śiva-Śakti). It also laid much emphasis upon the basic spirituality of Nature—of Nature inside man as well as Nature in the outside world. According to Tantra, in ultimate analysis, Nature is a mode of operation of the divine Spirit. So one must obtain a passport from Nature in order to enter into the kingdom of Spirit. If Nature binds man, she also liberates man. She alone can completely liberate man through his intelligent cooperation with her.

Emphasis on the basic spirituality of Nature naturally produces a bold affirmative attitude to life. The concept of *pravṛtti* (fulfillment of desires) sums up that affirmative attitude. The natural desires of man must not be suppressed or annihilated. They should be intelligently organized and lawfully satisfied. Therein lies the way of intelligent cooperation with Nature. Such cooperation alone can bestow upon man health and happiness, strength and beauty, growth and longevity. Moreover, as man learns to cooperate with Nature intelligently, Nature helps him to transcend her grosser forms and discover her finer forms. She helps him to rise above her lower material aspect and discover her higher spiritual aspect. The supernatural is the higher form and spiritual aspect of nature herself. Material Nature is the involved operation of Supernature, or the supernatural creative energy of the Spirit. So when man intelligently follows the guidance of nature, Nature herself unfolds before him in the fullness of time higher and higher spiritual values. With infinite care and patience, she guides him finally towards union with the eternal—with the formless essence of Being.

Now at the popular level, this healthy affirmative attitude of Tantra has often been misunderstood and misapplied. It has been construed as a go-ahead signal for unbridled gratification of the unconscious drives of human nature. In the guise of Tāntric religious practice, sexual promiscuity, drug addiction, cannibalism and gluttony etc. have often masqueraded.

Theistic schools, Vedāntic or Tāntric, could however never quite overcome the overall nondualistic framework of Indian thought. Buddha and Śankara stood as the two great giants presiding over the entire course of development of Indian culture during the middle ages. All other spiritual influences were like eddies and whirlpools in that mighty stream.

In the Bhagavad-Gītā a wonderful synthesis of nondualism and theism was attempted, a magnificent reconciliation of the transcendental and the cosmic aspects of Being was achieved. It was indicated how one can be united with the eternal and formless Being on the one hand and, on the other, participate in the creativity of the dynamic world-spirit. The Gītā pointed out that the formless eternity that transcends the world and the creative intelligence that sustains the world are two inseparable aspects of the same Being.

But medieval India was not quite ready for the grand synthesis, the master message of the Gītā. Consequently we find that each established school of theology got busy exploiting the Gītā as the vindication of its own creed. Each religious or metaphysical school tried to interpret the teaching of the Gītā as a stepping stone to its own specific ideal of liberation, supernaturalistic or transcendental.

Śankara Vedānta said that the Gītā's gospel of action and evolutionary participation was meant only for a particular caste of Hindu society, namely, the Kṣatriya. Other castes have a different role in society. Moreover the Gītā's emphasis upon action applies only to the preparatory stage of the spiritual aspirant. It is intended to purify a person through selfless action and thus qualify him for entrance into the final phase of renunciation and pure transcendental knowledge.

Theistic schools were eager to prove that the Gītā's message was only a stepping stone to the higher spiritual phase of supernatural love and devotion. Through social action one purifies one's nature. After that one is ready to direct the finer sentiments of the heart to the supernatural Deity. The ultimate goal is rapturous communion with the Divine from everlasting to everlasting in some transcendental abode of bliss and beatitude.

Direct confrontation with the evolutionary and historical dynamism of the modern West was needed for India to rediscover the integral outlook of the Gītā. And to rediscover with a deeper understanding the hidden treasures of the Vedas and Upaniṣads which are presented in dynamic form in the Gītā. Successive waves of foreign invasion drove the creative soul of India into a state of slumber. The shocking impact of revolutionary changes taking place in the outside world brought about her spiritual reawakening.

The great leaders of India's spiritual renaissance went back to the original teaching of the Vedas and Upaniṣads. Raja Rammohan, Sri Ramakrishna, Rabindranath Tagore, Swami Vivekananda, Swami Dayananda, Mahatma Gandhi, Sri Aurobindo—all of them harkened back to the mainsprings of Aryan culture. And all of them laid special emphasis upon the profound spiritual synthesis that shines through the pages of the Bhagavad-Gītā. The synthesis of spirit and life; of knowledge and action; of wisdom and compassion; of life transcendence and life participation; of world renunciation and world affirmation; of nondualistic vision of the eternal and dualistic appreciation of the struggle between truth and falsehood characteristic of human evolution.

From a renewed contact with the mainsprings of Indian culture, the leaders of renascent India came up with a very comprehensive outlook. They found that the distinctive values of East and West can be harmoniously blended within the framework of that outlook. We may call that the integral outlook. It has been the source of inspiration to the neo-Hindu and neo-Vedāntic movement in India. It stresses the need for a comprehensive philosophy of life as the foundation for integrated living, reconciling both material and spiritual values. It embodies a creative synthesis integrating the highest cultural values of East and West. It reconciles the economical, political, scientific and humanistic values of the modern West with the psychological, ontological and universal-religious values of the East.

Now no value synthesis can strike deep roots and become a dynamic force in society unless it is given adequate philosophic expression. It must be animated with a comprehensive and consistently thought-out world-view. Man is by his very nature metaphysical. He is at his best when he has a sense of purpose and a vision of destiny. He performs his noblest action when he has a grasp of the meaning of existence. And his sense of meaning and mission can flow only from an inspiring world-view. In our present age we need a world-view which takes into account the fundamental requirements of the age as well as the basic aspirations of man's evolving psyche. We need a world-view which shows how our deepest aspirations are related to the essential structure of the universe.

It was given to the great genius of Sri Aurobindo to outline the kind of comprehensive world-view which is essentially needed for the present age. The integral outlook which was germinally present in the Vedas and Upaniṣads, which became a dynamic force in the spiritual renaissance of India since early nineteenth century, received its complete philosophic expression in the writings of Sri Aurobindo. It gained a perfectly self-consistent and mature form, which may be designated integral nondualism. It incorporates the evolutionary perspective of the contemporary West into the nondualistic vision of the timeless and formless Being.

Thus the creative soul of India found a new voice in Sri Aurobindo. The great Indian poet Rabindranath

Tagore paid a visit to Sri Aurobindo at Pondicherry on February 16, 1928. He said to Sri Aurobindo, "You have the Word and we are waiting to receive it from you. India will speak through you, through your voice, harken unto me." The poet's words proved prophetic. Through Sri Aurobindo the soul of India has spoken to the world out of the accumulated wisdom of thousands of years. And it is a call to pool the cultural and spiritual resources of East and West toward the establishment of a unique world order on the spiritual foundation of creative freedom and integral truth-consciousness.

Chapter 3

INTEGRAL NONDUALISM

In the previous chapter we have seen that the integral worldview represents a comprehensive philosophical synthesis. It reconciles the nondualistic outlook of the East with the evolutionary perspective of the modern West. It may therefore be aptly described as integral nondualism. It is nondualism in dynamic form. In imparting to nondualism an evolutionary orientation, it activates the creative potential of eastern mysticism. Whereas traditional mysticism aims at the liberation of union with the eternal, integral nondualism impregnates that union with a dynamic vision of the future.

In order to grasp fully the significance of integral nondualism as a supreme East-West synthesis, it might be desirable to have some precise understanding of traditional nondualism in its purest form. Is it true to say that nondualism (advaita) is a uniquely distinctive feature of eastern culture? Is not nondualism present also in western culture in the shape of monotheism, monism, pantheism, etc?

The purpose of this chapter is to show how nondualism in its pure form is different from monism, monotheism, pantheism and the like. In spite of considerable resemblance, nondualism differs from the latter in some essential respects. Nondualism in its pure form is India's very unique contribution to the spiritual heritage of man. An adequate grasp of it is essentially needed to lay a stable philosophical and spiritual foundation for abiding world peace and human progress.

The fundamental requirement of our present age is to enlarge and enrich the nondualistic outlook with a creative sense of history. A harmonious blending of eastern nondualism and western historicism can provide a comprehensive philosophy of life such as can inspire the future progress of civilization. Traditional nondualism (advaita) must be dynamically reoriented so that India may play her role effectively in the march of world affairs. On the other side evolutionism and historicism must be nondualistically founded so that creative energies of the West may be peacefully channeled in the interest of total human welfare.

What is Monotheism?

What is monotheism? Monotheism is the religious belief in one personal God. It rejects the polytheistic faith in many gods and goddesses. The one personal God which monotheism affirms is endowed with certain well defined attributes and powers such as justice, mercy, wisdom, love, etc. He is believed to be the living embodiment of a determinate combination of certain social, ethical, and religious values. It is further believed that it is only by accepting such a determinate conception of God that people can attain salvation.

The great merit of monotheism lies in its unifying and organizing power. A well-knit organization requires some well defined organizing principle. It requires unquestioning faith in a fixed set of values. One God, one prophet or messiah, one book of revelation—that is the great formula of an organized religious fraternity. Exactly such a triple formula is applied by monotheism.

The chief defect of monotheism is that it tends to make its followers dogmatic, intolerant and aggressive. The one God of monotheism is endowed with some definable powers and attributes. These are crystallized in definite dogmas and creeds which are believed to represent the absolute truth. Those who do not accept these dogmas and creeds are branded as heretics and atheists. The faithful feel religiously justified to persecute the latter. They feel justified to wage a holy war against the infidels and nonbelievers. Such persecution and holy crusades are not only justified on religious grounds; they are even considered a supreme religious duty, a divine commandment. Thus hatred and hostility, violence and inquisition, crusade and conversion, are paradoxically born of one's faith in one loving and merciful God.

Monotheism is oftener than not dualistic in outlook from the metaphysical standpoint. It believes in one God, but it usually imagines the world to have an inferior mode of existence outside of God, the most high and perfect. God is the upholder of the supernatural kingdom of heaven. In the heavenly region, He is surrounded by a graded hierarchy of angels. The world is the abode of sin and suffering, of trial and tribulation. It is the place of punishment for the violation of the Divine Will. It is the prison-house for those who fall from divine grace by eating the forbidden apple.

The oneness of God is thus compromised, metaphysically speaking, by the separate existence of the world as a realm of evil and imperfection. It is also compromised by the separate existence of the devil or Satan. The devil frequently challenges the authority of God and foils His noble designs. There ensues thus a continuous struggle between the forces of God and the forces of the devil in the benighted world of imperfection.

The dualism of God and world makes the followers of monotheism otherworldly and supernaturalistic. Nature is regarded as the antithesis of spirit. Religious striving assumes the form of a perpetual struggle between the flesh and the spirit, between passion and reason. It encourages a rebellion against the natural order in one's search for the supernatural.

The dualism of God and the devil generates an aggressive and proselytizing zeal in the ranks of the faithful.

Those who do not accept the right creed—the only creed that represents the will of God—must be under the spell of the devil. So they must be either converted or crushed in order to win the world over to God. Thus the followers of different monotheistic systems may find themselves locked in a mortal combat, each side fighting in the name of one absolute God. The God of each monotheistic system becomes, therefore, the devil in relationship to the God of the other system. And those who do not believe in God at all, the atheists and agnostics, must be doubly accursed, incorrigibly corrupted by the devil's devil.

Philosophical reflection exposes in no time the self-contradiction inherent in monotheism in its popular form. If God is one, infinite and absolute, He cannot exist outside of and beyond the world. God must be the One all-embracing and all-pervading Spirit. There cannot also be any devil existing separately outside of God. The devil, if there should be one, must somehow be an integral part of the existence of the absolute Godhead, functioning as the dialectical element in His objective self-manifestation.

In other words, if God is infinite, the world must exist within God, not outside Him. God must be omnipresent and all-encompassing, not a supernatural Other. One must at least be able to say that God is both immanent and transcendent. On the one hand God is the great Beyond, and on the other He is the inner life and the controlling power of the entire universe. But, in consequence of such a modification, monotheism gets transformed into monistic theism or theistic monism. It becomes a religious version of the monistic worldview. For the sake of full clarity, it would be good at this time to say a word about monism.

What is Monism?

Monism as a philosophical world-view holds that the world, with all its bewildering variety of things and beings, is the offspring of one universal creative principle.

Monism further proceeds to endow this universal principle with a determinate character. Different ways of con-
ceiving the one supreme principle give rise to different
systems of monism.

The universal creative principle may be conceived as
matter or material energy. That would establish material-
istic monism. It may be conceived as one universal life-
force. That would establish vitalistic monism. It may be
conceived as one universal Mind or Reason. That would
establish idealistic monism. It may be conceived as one
all-embracing and all-transcending personal God, endowed
with such attributes as all-powerful, all-wise, all-good, all-
merciful, etc. That would establish theistic monism.

Transition To Pantheism

Further philosophical reflection detects self-contradiction inherent in monism. In Western philosophy, a cri-
tique of monism prepared the ground for pantheism,
panentheism and absolutism. These are the closest parallels in the West to what is known as nondualism in the
East. Eastern nondualism is embodied in such systems as
Advaita Vedānta, Kāṣmīr Śaivism, Mahāyāna Buddhism,
Taoism and Zen. Western pantheism, with slight variations, is embodied in the great speculative systems of
Plotinus, Spinoza, Bradley, Bosanquet, etc.

Spinoza's formulation of pantheism is classical. In his
view, the ultimate ground of existence is one infinite
substance. We cannot limit this infinite substance by
ascribing to it a specific combination of determinate qualities as theism does. Because to determine is to limit. All
determinatio est negatio. So God as the infinite substance
must be either void of all attributes or endowed with
infinite attributes, embracing and reconciling such human
opposites as love and hate, joy and sorrow, good and evil,
etc.

Of the infinite attributes of God, two are especially
known to us human beings, namely consciousness and ex-

tension. These are parallel manifestations of the Divine Essence. Corresponding to every conscious process there is the material process, and vice versa. Other attributes of God are unknown to the average human being at his present stage of growth. Different material objects are modifications of one God as extended. Different finite *spirits* are modifications of God as conscious. So God is absolutely immanent in the all of existence. God is identical in the world of nature and man.

The German philosopher Krause coined the word panentheism by way of suggesting an improvement upon Spinoza's pantheism. Pantheism means all is God. This makes God absolutely immanent in the world, and thus ignores His transcendental aspect as the great Beyond. Panentheism means all is *in* God. This implies that God embraces and pervades the entire universe, and at the same time transcends it as the inexhaustible and the unmanifest. In pantheism finite spirits are modes of God's infinite consciousness. Consequently they have no independent existence and real freedom of their own. In panentheism finite spirits are relatively independent substances endowed with a relative measure of freedom, even though for all their freedom and independence, they still live, move and have their being within the all-embracing medium of divine existence.

Such absolutist philosophers as Hegel, Bradley and Bosanquet tried to reform pantheism in another direction. If the ultimate ground of existence is not to be identified with any fixed set of determinations, as Spinoza rightly points out, then it is not proper to call it God. God is a specifically religious category. God is the sovereign personal Being endowed with certain ethical and religious attributes. The personal God of religion must therefore be only an appearance, a phenomenal manifestation, of the Absolute. The Absolute—the truly infinite and eternal Being—must transcend all theological determinations, that is to say, all dogmas and creeds expressing determinate characteristics of God.

Moreover, Spinoza's notion of the one, infinite, inde-terminate substance is self-contradictory. If the One is indeterminable, then how can we determine It by the category of substance? Substance—attribute is the category of the human mind. It is man's imperfect way of arrang-ing the manifold facts of experience. It applies, therefore, only to the realm of phenomenal appearances. It cannot be extended, as Immanuel Kant pointed out, to ultimate reality. So Bradley concludes that ultimate reality is the logically indefinable system of all experience. Multitud-inous phenomena that we experience—appearances as the facts of experience—are the stuff of which the Absolute is made. The Absolute unifies and transforms them all. But It has no assets beyond appearances.[1] The notion of the Beyond contradicts the fundamental idealistic premise that all is experience. Anything beyond experience is an empty hypothesis.

The Essence of Nondualism

As we noted before, pantheism, panentheism and ab-solutism are Western parallels to Indian nondualism. But nondualism cannot be quite equated with any of them. It has some distinctive features of its own which have yet to be investigated.

Buddha and Śankara are the two most consistent expo-nents in India of nondualism in its purest and highest form. The key concept of Sankara is formless Being (*Nirguna Brahman*). The key concept of Buddha is Non-being (Śūnyatā). From the spiritual standpoint, Being and Nonbeing are identical. There is no doubt that there are many differences between the teachings of these two great masters. But underlying such differences there is a profound measure of agreement. They agree in affirming the concept of pure Transcendence as the indefinable and nontemporal depth dimension of all existence. And that is an essential ingredient of nondualism.

---

[1] F. H. Bradley, *Appearance and Reality* (London: Oxford University Press, 1962). p. 433.

Neither pantheism nor panentheism is quite the same as pure nondualism. The word "Theos" signifies God. Now God is a Being endowed with ethical and religious attributes. God is therefore a determinate form of Being. He is *a* Being, not the ground of *all* being. So He cannot be equated with Being as such. Being in its inmost essence is indeterminable and formless. Indeterminable Being is not to be interpreted as one infinite substance. The notion of one infinite substance is an intellectual construction. The mystery of Being can hardly be fathomed by such categories of the intellect as substance, quality, unity, plurality, etc.

The absolutism of Bradley and Bosanquet also falls short of pure nondualism. Absolutism is right in holding that ultimate reality is beyond one and many, beyond substance and quality, beyond immediate experience and rational mediation. But there are at least two essential respects in which nondualism differs from it.

First, western absolutism shows no full comprehension of the aspect of Being as supracosmic transcendence. The reason probably lies in the fact that philosophers like Bradley and Bosanquet, for all their intellectual brilliance, had no firsthand mystical realization. Bradley states that appearances are the stuff of which the Absolute is made. "The Absolute has no assets beyond appearances."[2] This is like saying that the ocean has no assets beyond the waves. Or like saying that the space-time continuum has no assets beyond visible and tangible material objects. To say that the Absolute means only the transmuted unity of all appearances is to betray a lack of understanding of the nontemporal depth dimension of the universe. The ocean is much more than the transmuted unity of its waves.

Secondly, in declaring that ultimate reality is the Absolute, Bradley and Bosanquet suggest that ultimate reality must be a rationally self-coherent system. It was difficult for them to shake off the hang-over from Hegelian rationalism. Did not Hegel say that all that is real is rational,

---

[2] Ibid. p. 433.

and all that is rational is real? So the principle of self-consistency must be the ultimate criterion of truth. Ultimate reality must be, on the one hand, all-inclusive, and, on the other, rationally self-coherent. In one word, it must be a *system*.

But according to nondualism, Being is beyond all systems. Different systems, that is, intellectually constructed wholes, are only different perspectives of the fullness of Being. It is true that Being has an aspect of harmony and consistency. But it is no less true that there is an irrational factor in the structure of reality. There is in life an irreducible surd which just won't lend itself to any rational deduction. This is what Vedānta calls *māyā*. The absolutist's claim that his philosophical system is absolutely true from the intellectual standpoint is false. All philosophical systems are only relatively valid from a particular standpoint, at a given stage of evolution. Only the formless Being is absolute. But the formless Being is the common source of inspiration to all metaphysical systems, monistic, pluralistic, dualistic and otherwise.

Ancient nondualism at its best, as we find it in the teachings of Buddha and Śankara, represents mysticism at its loftiest. Theistic, pantheistic and other forms of mysticism are pale reflections thereof. The core of nondualistic mysticism lies in the conviction that the supreme truth is the timeless and formless Being or Nonbeing. Reality is essentially indefinable and nonverbal. It is beyond all opposites—nondual. Beyond all limitations of cosmic expression, it is still the source and support of the cosmic manifold.

A Hindu theistic mystic may say, "I am at one with Kṛṣṇa." Insofar as he is a theist, and not a nondualist in the strict sense of the word, he finds it difficult to rise above the Kṛṣṇa-form. Indeterminable Being is for him only an abstraction. At best it is the limitless power and glory of the determinate Kṛṣṇa-form. Similarly, a Christian mystic, who is usually a theist, says, "I am at one with Christ, or with God the Father, who is inseparable from Christ." He finds it extremely difficult to rise above the Christ-form and comprehend Being in its transcendent-universal essence. He cannot think of Being apart from Christ, nor can he approach Being except through Christ. Similarly, an Islamic mystic, insofar as he is a theist, says, "I am at one with the essence of Mohammed." He finds it difficult to rise above the Mohammed-form. All theists, Hindu, Jewish, Christian, Islamic, etc., find it difficult to shake loose from the dualistic conception of God as *a* Being, a sovereign Person, and comprehend what Paul Tillich calls Being itself, the ground of all being. It is Being itself, the *tathatā* or suchness of Mahāyāna Buddhism, and indeterminable Being (Nirguṇa Brahman) of Advaita Vedānta, which is the ultimate category of non-dualism.

When a nondualist says "I am in essence one with formless Being," he goes beyond all forms and determinations and reaches the rock-bottom realization of Being as such in its boundless universality. Formless Being is the common ground of all such specific symbols of the Divine, as Kṛṣṇa, Buddha, Christ, Mohammed, Moses, etc., with all their historical particularities. The latter represent historical forms of the transhistorical reality. The theist equates the historical form with the transhistorical. Consequently the transhistorical reality appears to him as a person. Failure to rise above personalities and to comprehend the superpersonal divine ground introduces an element of parochialism into his religious outlook. He fails to appreciate the common universal essence of all religions. He sets up one religion against other religions, one particular prophet above all other prophets. Nondualistic experience of Being-itself can alone discover the ultimate unity of all prophets and all religions, resulting in a genuine universality of outlook. Short of that, some degree of religious narrow-mindedness is bound to remain. Pure nondualism is a spiritual breakthrough beyond all limitations of dogma and creed. It is the experience of Being in its formless essence and all-comprehensive unity.

Integral Nondualism

Let us now raise the final question: How does Integral nondualism differ from the nondualism of Buddha and Śankara? Is it a restatement of Vedāntic-Buddhist nondualism in modern terms? Or has it any unique and distinctive features of its own?

Integral nondualism differs from ancient nondualism at least in two essential respects.

Integral nondualism transforms ancient nondualism into an affirmative and dynamic attitude to life by incorporating into it the evolutionary perspective. Ancient nondualism aims at ecstatic union with the eternal. Integral Nondualism is dynamic and creative union with the eternal.

Secondly, integral nondualism affirms Being as the undivided unity of the formless and multiple forms. According to ancient nondualism, ultimate reality is the formless, the indeterminable. Forms and determinations are unreal from the ultimate standpoint. In the view of integral nondualism, forms and determinations also are very real from the ultimate standpoint. They are the glory of the creative urge inherent in Being. They provide meaning and reality to the self-expressive impulse of Being. If we are to use a human analogy, the formless corresponds to the creative depth, the boundless potentiality, of a master artist. Different forms inhere in the determinate works of art accomplished by his genius. We know that his finished products of art are no less real than his inarticulate and as yet unmanifest inner vision.

In the Vedāntic-Buddhist spiritual tradition, dominant emphasis is upon the formless Being. Names and forms (nāma-rūpa) are unreal (mithyā). Unreal because they are ever-changing, ephemeral, evanescent (anitya). In contrast to this denial of forms and names, it was given to the genius of ancient Greek philosophers like Plato and Aristotle to emphasize the reality of names and forms. According to Plato, particular things and beings are no doubt ever changing and perishing, but their essential forms (Ideas) are eternally real. They are the formative principles of things. They are the archetypal models of existence. Forms and ideas are indeed supremely real. Concepts and definitions are real insofar as they are the structural principles of things. Thus Plato's doctrine of ideas laid the groundwork for a different line of cultural development from the Oriental mystical tradition. In the fullness of time it gave rise to the approach of precise scientific formulation and logical articulation. It stressed the need for the organized way of doing things according to definite principles and ideologies. Science's emphasis upon mathematical formulation and well defined laws as the essence of things is the logical culmination of the Platonic doctrine of ideas. The gradual perfecting, in the West, of social and political institutions has also been, in a large measure, due to the rationalistic regard for determinate forms as structural elements of reality.

Integral nondualism reconciles the mystical truth of formless Being with the rationalistic theory of forms and ideas. It holds that it is wrong to identify reality exclusively with formless transcendence. Forms and ideas are no less real. Formless transcendence on the one hand, and eternal forms and ideas on the other, may be said to represent two equally real dimensions of Being. Realization of the formless transcendence is essential for attaining spiritual depth and universality of outlook, whereas realization of the reality and value of forms, ideas, determinate principles, etc., is essential for human progress in scientific, technological, social, economical and political spheres. The former is necessary for world peace and harmony. The latter is necessary for the gradual improvement of human institutions, and for continuous betterment of the conditions of living in this world.

Integral nondualism reconciles mysticism with evolutionism. Mystics affirm the reality of the nontemporal depth dimension of Being. Realization of the nontemporal is essential for supreme peace and serenity, for wisdom and universal compassion, for the authentic spirit of universal brotherhood free of any master-race or master-creed complex. But ancient mysticism was not fully aware of the reality and importance of evolution and history. Dazzled by the glory of the eternal, it minimized the importance and value of time. Attracted by the bliss of the timeless present, it lost the historic vision of the future.

The theory of evolution upholds an optimistic vision of the future. It calls attention to the supreme reality of life as a creative process. It stresses the truth that man's reality cannot be separated from his historicity. It is through participation in history that he can evolve and manifest the unsuspected glories of his inner being. Integral nondualism holds that the nontemporal and the evolutionary are two inseparable aspects of Being. The nontemporal is the formless depth of Being. The evolutionary is the creative energy (*Śakti*) inherent in Being. So by enlarging the concept of energy (*Śakti*) or determinate Being (*Saguṇa Brahman*), which is already there in Vedānta, mysticism and evolutionism can be perfectly reconciled.

It follows from the above that man, who is a self-conscious mode of expression of Being, has also two inseparable aspects. On the one hand he has the formless and timeless depth dimension of his existence. He needs to realize this in order to attain peace, wisdom, freedom and love in their perfection. But, on the other hand, he has the historical dimension of his being. He is born in a specific historical context and part of his ultimate goal of life lies in playing an active role in the march of history. It is no doubt by diving into the depths of his being that he can glimpse life's supreme values. But it is by actively participating in the evolutionary movement of life that he can increasingly manifest higher values in society and human relations.

Chapter 4

EXISTENTIALISM AND RATIONALISM

Existentialism is a very significant form of the philosophical movement in the West today. It is a protest against the traditional rationalism and rationalistic idealism of Western culture. It is also a protest against traditional religiosity in the form of supernaturalism, pessimism, and otherworldliness.

Existentialism has rendered a signal service to modern man in his search for truth. It has cleared away a good deal of mythological speculation and meaningless verbiage. It has shaken the foundation of rationalistic castle building inspired by the dogma that the real is the rational. But in doing so it commits excesses of its own, equating reality with the absurd, the irrational.

It is indeed important to be able to know the truth in its naked form, however overwhelming the experience. But it is also essential to comprehend the truth in its total form—in its integral fullness—however painstaking the effort. Integral philosophy is an attempt to present the truth in its multidimensional fullness. In doing so it brings together in a balanced outlook the refreshing insights of existentialism on the one hand and the imperishable values of rationalism and idealism on the other.

Thought and Existence

Traditional speculative philosophy affirms the primacy of thought as the vehicle of truth. Existentialism affirms the subordination of thought to existence as the fundamental structure of reality. Integral philosophy holds that thought and existence are interdependent modes of expression of the same timeless Being (Brahman).

Descartes says: "I think therefore I am; cogito ergo sum." He starts with thought. Existence is revealed through thought. Naturally therefore thought is regarded as the essence of existence. And existence is understood in terms of such categories of thought as substance, permanence, cause, unity, etc. So the human reality is conceived as a permanent thinking substance ontologically separate from the body. The puzzles and problems stemming from such dualistic thinking are common knowledge today. The insoluble problem of interaction between the body and the soul, matter and mind, is artificially created. It opens the door to skepticism, solipsism, and the world-negating flights of idealism.

Once thought is accepted as the vehicle of truth, the ground is prepared for the eventual enthronement of thought as the absolute. So rationalism reaches its ultimate fulfillment in absolute idealism. And this is what precisely happened in Hegel's philosophy. Hegel draws the ultimate inevitable conclusion from the Cartesian premise. For Hegel, all that is real is rational, and all that is rational is real. Thought is identical with ultimate reality. The supreme truth is absolute idea, an organic structure of the categories of thought. Nature can be derived from absolute idea as a form of its objective self-manifestation or self-externalization. Human existence also can be derived from absolute idea seeking self-expression in and through the evolutionary movement of nature. The existing individual becomes thus an image or reproduction of the Hegelian absolute. He is a shadow cast by the light of absolute thought. His destiny therefore lies in losing himself in the absolute. In the political field his destiny lies in losing himself in the state as a concrete manifestation on earth of the absolute. Thus we see how rationalism can lead to absolute idealism and how absolute idealism can prepare the way for Nazism, Fascism, Statism and political dictatorship.

This whole line of thinking comes in for sharp criticism at the hands of modern existentialist thinkers. What is needed is a complete reversal of the rationalistic premise. "I am, therefore I think"—that would sum up the fundamental existentialist position. Existence cannot be derived from thought and its categories. On the contrary, thought is a mere function of existence. Besides thought, existence involves such nonrationalistic factors as immediate sense experience, emotion, love, action, intuition, etc. Moreover the existence of every human individual is an ultimate irreducible fact. It is unique, and incapable of duplication. The individual is just the individual.

Jean-Paul Sartre has drawn the ultimate logical conclusion from the existentialist emphasis upon the uniqueness of the existing individual—an emphasis which started with Soren Kierkegaard in modern times. If the individual is an ultimate unit of existence, he must be absolutely free. His freedom can know no bounds. It cannot be limited by any ethical standard or norm. Nor should it be limited by any social or political authority. Nor should it be curbed by any religious injunction. Whatever flows from the individual's exercise of absolute freedom must be good. Free choice is the essential criterion of goodness. Free choice is also the key to the understanding of individuality.

Be it noted, however, that absolute freedom when carried to the extreme, turns into its opposite, bondage. Just as indeterminate being is, as Hegel taught, indistinguishable from nothing, so also free choice without any sense of purpose or guidance of value, is indistinguishable from whimsical chaos. The freedom of unrestrained self-indulgence leads to the tyranny of inner compulsion. Lawless liberty turns into helpless licentiousness.

In society it is the goal of collective good that turns the energy of freedom into humanitarian action. It is the rule of law that diverts liberty from suicidal clash to the path of constructive cooperation. In individual life it is the goal of authentic self-realization and the discipline of purposive self-organization that impart meaning and value to the freedom of self-expression. Thus it becomes very clear that freedom and discipline, liberty and law, are inseparable aspects of man's search for the supreme good.

According to integral philosophy neither can thought be derived from existence nor can existence be derived from thought. If existence in a sense transcends thought, thought also in a sense transcends existence. If thought is dependent upon existence in some respect, existence also is dependent upon thought in some respect. Both thought and existence are closely interrelated modes of manifestation of the cosmic creative energy (Śakti) of the timeless Being (Brahman).

The existing human individual is a unique focalized expression of Being. The physical basis of his existence is provided by the highly developed nervous system crowned by that specific constellation of neurons known as the cerebrum. It is a wonderful instrument of intelligent communication with the outside world, an amazingly flexible responsiveness to the changing circumstances of life. It is the locus of a large variety of unconscious instinctual drives, functional dispositions and creative urges.

But the greatest of all miracles is that the human organism is characterized by consciousness. Consciousness (Cit) is indeed of the essence of human reality. It is coextensive with existence. Descartes was in a sense right in emphasizing consciousness as the defining characteristic of the human spirit. But his big mistake was the mistake of rationalism which equates consciousness with rationality and reflective thinking. The truth is that consciousness is a much wider category than rational thinking.

The word consciousness can be accepted as the defining characteristic of existence when it is used in a broad comprehensive sense including nonreflective as well as reflective modes of awareness. Consciousness covers different levels of awareness and insight. It implies the intuitive insights of the unconscious mind and the purposiveness of instinctual drives. It implies the awareness characteristic of dream states. It implies the witness consciousness present even in the condition of deep sleep. In deep sleep the waking mind does indeed go out of action. There may be little or no dreaming. But still there is a sort of unobjective consciousness. That is why after a period of deep dreamless sleep, a person is in a position to remark that he had a very peaceful sleep which he enjoyed.

Then there is an element of consciousness in states of swoon and hypnosis in drug-induced trance and hallucination (e.g. hallucination produced by LSD, mescalin, etc.). The ordinary waking consciousness is blacked out. Strange fascinating experiences may keep pouring in. Or a person may find himself tormented by hellish experiences. He may feel helplessly in the grip of uncontrollable forces. But still deep within himself there is an element of consciousness taking note of what is happening. Ancient mythology testifies to the presence of this deep-seated witness consciousness in man. In the course of his adventures Ulysses reached the charmed island of Circe. His men were converted by Circe into swine. They were absolutely helpless to do anything about this degrading metamorphosis. But still they knew what was happening and by virtue of this fact that the light of consciousness was kept alive inside them, the hope of redemption was not lost. They were again liberated into human form.

The word consciousness also signifies the light of transcendental consciousness. By the power of consciousness a man can always make a new unpredictable decision in a new situation. He can thus stultify all predictions about his behavior pattern. He can rise above the determinism of his impulses and instincts. He can also rise above his social and political circumstances. With reckless abandon he may prefer death to capitulation to the enemy. Thus the self-transcending power of consciousness brings to man a boundless measure of freedom.

Consciousness also implies man's discovery of the spiritual dimension of his being. By virtue of consciousness, for all his finitude, he can glimpse the reality of the infinite. Despite his imperfection, he can envision the glory of perfection. For all his transience and contingency of life, he can contact the non-temporal basis of existence. However much he may be torn by the discords and discrepancies of life, the vision comes to him of higher and higher values inspiring him to selfless deeds of love and sacrifice at the altar of truth, beauty and human welfare. Finally, it is by virtue of consciousness that man gains insight into the scheme of cosmic evolution of which he is an integral part. He has a deep sense of fulfillment from intelligent cooperation with the creative force of evolution. Consciousness thus becomes the most dynamic form of self-fulfillment through self-transcendence. It is the power of nature brought to self-awareness in man. The creativity of nature acquires in him a new dimension of self-expression.

In the light of the above discussion we are now in a position to understand better the mutuality of existence and consciousness. Consciousness depends upon existence, because without the evolutionary growth of man's nervous system consciousness as we know it in man would not have come into being. It is a unique emergent value. It is a novel characteristic which emerges into being on the perfecting of the human cerebral structure. But consciousness also transcends existence, because it reveals the cosmic whole as it essentially is. It reveals the eternal as it timelessly is. It glimpses the grandeur of Being as pure transcendence. It is the vision of the eternal which inspires the individual to deeds of sacrifice and love.

On the other hand it may be said that existence is dependent upon consciousness. For man is born not as a finished product but as an unfinished task. Animals are born as fixed types of nature. But the human body is born as the most helpless creature in the world. But it is precisely in this weakness that man's glory lies. His initial helplessness stems from the fact that he is born with the most flexible nervous system. It can be shaped and moulded in an endless variety of ways. It can adjust and readjust itself to most revolutionary changes in the environment. In other words, man is born with a rich promise and a boundless potential. He is born with the freedom to recreate himself in the image of perfection he carries in his heart. He is born with a very responsible task—that of finishing nature's unfinished job—the task of becoming man. Whereas animals are born as animals, men are born with the free potentiality of becoming men. And that potentiality is indeed immeasurable. Consciousness is awareness of this task, of man's boundless freedom and potentiality. The more consciousness evolves, the more existence becomes what it potentially is.

But existence also in a sense transcends consciousness. The consciousness of an individual has no doubt the power to go beyond the individual and to cognize the outside world and the infinite. But with all this power of going beyond it, it is still the self-transcending characteristic of the existing individual. It presupposes the existence of the individual as its solid foundation. And paradoxically enough, by virtue of this very self-transcending power of consciousness, existence, far from being abrogated, is more and more enriched. It becomes more and more of existence. It becomes more and more individuated by its vision of the supraindividual. Therefore the perfect individual is he who discovers the universal in his life. The richest and most colorful individual is he who surrenders to the eternal and learns to refashion his whole being in the light of the eternal.

How can this paradoxical fact be understood? How can existence and consciousness which seem to go beyond each other be still interdependent facets of the same living individual? The paradox of the situation can be comprehended when we remember that the individual is, in ultimate analysis, a unique center of self-expression of Being. Being is on the one hand cosmic energy and on the other formless eternity. Man's concrete nervous system is a specific creation of cosmic energy. Consciousness which emerges into being as a characteristic of the nervous system reflects the self-luminosity of timeless and formless Being. The self-light of the formless Being, when reflected upon the animal level, may be called the unconscious. When reflected upon the average human brain, it is consciousness. When developed in man to the limit of its power, when expanded to the dimensions of the universe, it may be called by some such name as cosmic consciousness, unitive consciousness, undivided and unobjective consciousness, etc. But the self-light of the formless Being (or the creative void) as it is in itself is an unfathomable mystery to which even the word cosmic consciousness would perhaps be inadequate. Whereas consciousness is an emergent value, the self-light of the eternal is the primordial reality.

Sri Aurobindo's word Superconscience[1] is perhaps better descriptive of that mysterious self-light of Being. It is the source of higher and higher levels of consciousness emerging in the course of inner evolution. In itself it is beyond both existence and consciousness. It is beyond both nature and spirit. It is beyond both matter and mind. But by virtue of cosmic energy—the evolutionary urge of Being—Being is manifested in the form of all manner of dualities.

---

[1] Sri Aurobindo, *The Life Divine* (Pondicherry: Sri Aurobindo Ashram, 1955), p. 379.

Chapter 5

EXISTENTIALISM AND ESSENTIALISM

One of the most salient features of man's rational consciousness is its ability to transcend the sense impressions of the passing moment. The animal mind is immersed in the flux of sensuous immediacy. Guided by instinct, it responds to the stimulus of momentary sense data. But the human mind can look beyond the immediacy of sensuous prehension. It can grasp universals. It can cognize the common and essential characteristics that bind together in a single class multitudinous particulars. It can contemplate what Plato called archetypal ideas, essences, forms.

For instance, a dog sensuously apprehends different human beings that approach him in their particularity. He is not reflectively aware of the qualitative essence characteristic of all human beings. Man's reflective awareness of the essence of man liberates him from the particularity of sensuous immediacy. It enables him to build up increasing knowledge about the behavior patterns of the human race. It enables him to extract valuable information from his experiences of the past in human relations. It enables him also to anticipate and predict human behavior within certain limits.

In short it is the rational comprehension of universal essences and forms—of Platonic Ideas—which has played a significant role in the growth of civilization. It lays the foundation for the understanding of causal connections between phenomena. It initiates chains of reasoning leading from the present to the past and the future, from the observed to the unobserved, from the known to the unknown. The development of science is ultimately traceable to the comprehension of pure essences and their interrelationships. Plato's doctrine of Ideas, modified in some respects, laid the ground work for precise formulation of the laws of science. Only the essences are no longer conceived in science as self-subsistent entities beyond the realm of phenomena. On the contrary, they are understood as tools or instruments of rational comprehension. They have no reality apart from phenomena. They acquire reality by "being ingredient" in phenomena or the passage of events, as Whitehead puts it.

In art also a clear vision of significant forms or structural patterns performs a very important function. It is by arranging a multiplicity of sense impressions within the unity of the structural design that the artist creates harmony and beauty. The sensuous manifold is the mere chaos. Order is brought out of such chaos by the ordering power of some significant form that is revealed to the artist's mind.

It was the comprehension of universal essences which was also responsible for the evolution of thought in religion and philosophy.

Existentialism and Essentialism

The concept or essence of matter serves as the unifying principle of the whole class of material phenomena. The concept or essence of mind serves as the unifying principle of the whole class of mental or psychological phenomena. The concept or essence of life serves as the unifying principle of the whole class of biological phenomena. Now, both religion and philosophy are motivated by the search for the unity beyond all such unities—for the ultimate unifying principle of the entire universe composed of matter, life and mind. It is believed that the ultimate unity must be the Essence of all essences, the Universal of all universals. Religion calls it God. Philosophy calls it the Absolute.

In medieval times universals were conceived as self-subsistent reals. The sensuous world of actual entities or existing particulars was believed derived from the self-subsistent realm of eternal Ideas or Essences. Ideas or Essences in turn were believed to be unified in God. God was affirmed as the Idea of all Ideas, or as the universal Mind to which all Ideas owe their reality and interrelations. Thus the notion of God as the self-existent unity of all Ideas provided the ultimate principle of explanation for the entire universe of nature and man.

Philosophy perceives self-contradiction in the religious notion of God. God conceived as a self-existent spiritual substance or Person is recognized as a particular entity, however omniscient and omnipotent. He fails as the universal Essence or Idea that he must be in order to function as the ultimate unifying principle of the world. He becomes a "Primus inter pares," or "an each among eaches," as William James puts it. Such a God, for all his sovereignty, can hardly function as the ultimate principle of unity.

So philosophy carries its search for unity beyond the Personal God of religion. In doing so rationalistic philosophy develops the notion of the Absolute as the systematic unity of all Ideas, Forms and Essences. It was given to Hegel to draw this conclusion in its logical perfection. The Absolute is, in the view of Hegel, Absolute Idea, the organic unity of all ideas and categories. Everything in heaven and earth can be explained as a mode of objective self-expression of the Absolute Idea. Nature is Idea in the form of self-estrangement.[1] History is the process of accomplishing what is in essence eternally accomplished. "The Good, the absolutely Good . . . needs not wait upon us, but is already by implication, as well as in full actuality, accomplished." It is an "illusion which makes it seem yet unaccomplished."[2]

---

[1] Hegel, *Encyclopedia of Philosophy*, Gustav Emil Mueller trans. (New York: Philosophical Library, 1959), p. 166.

[2] William Wallace trans., *The Logic of Hegel* (London: Oxford University Press, 1892), p. 352.

But the Idea of Hegel, however absolute, is no better than an abstraction of thought—the abstraction of all abstractions. It is the most all-inclusive of all abstractions. For all its infinitude in the realm of abstraction it has not the power to create or explain a single infinitesimal particle of matter or process of mind. If the religious notion of Personal God errs on the side of particularity, the philosophic notion of Absolute Idea errs on the side of abstract universality. A personal god is too much of a particular existent to serve as the ultimate unifying principle of the world. The absolute idea is too much of an abstract universal to explain the existence of the actual world. It only sums up the categorical features, the structural characteristics, of the actual world.

The importance of the present day existentialist movement lies in its rejection of the priority of essence over existence. All attempts to derive existence from essence are foredoomed to failure for the simple reason that existence is existence. Existence is irreducible fact incapable of being resolved into non-existential terms. "What-is is" as Martin Heidegger says.[3] It cannot be resolved into a complex of essences. It cannot be reduced to a tissue of bloodless categories. The mystery of Being cannot be fathomed in terms of concepts and laws, however elaborately formulated. Human reality is not a deterministic scheme. It transcends all definable laws. It has the freedom to burst through all bonds of determinism, social, economical, political and theological. Existential freedom brooks no limitation from any quarter. Neither from the state, nor from the will of a personal god. That is why tyranny in any form, political or theological, sows the seed of its own destruction by provoking eventual rebellion or revolution.

Now the point to be noted here is that every protest movement commits an excess of its own. Existentialism is right in pointing out that existence cannot be derived from essence, or that the realm of actuality cannot be de-

---

[3] Martin Heidegger, *Existence and Being* (Chicago: Henry Regnery Co., 1949), p. 386.

rived from the realm of ideas. Existence precedes essence, as Jean-Paul Sartre puts it. But it seems to us that in exposing the cosmological pretension of essentialism, the existentialist philosopher makes the grievous mistake of ignoring the value of ideas, essences, and universals in the structure of reality. It is like throwing the baby away with the bath water.

Let us make the point clear again. Existence cannot certainly be derived from essence. But at the same time it must not be forgotten that essences form a vital factor in the meaning of existence. True, the particular existent is not a mere complex of universals or ideas. But at the same time it must not be forgotten that ideas provide the key to our understanding of the structure of the existing individual in his relationship to the universe. They embody the structural elements in the scheme of existence.

Essences or ideas become real only as they are ingredient in the actual existence of the world. They are the defining characteristics of all objects and events. They are the differentiating features of the flux of phenomena. What integral philosophy wishes especially to emphasize in this connection is that there is an important sense in which both essence and existence are unified in the structure of Being. They are two inseparable aspects of Being.

Existing individuals certainly cannot be resolved into essences. Nor can they be accepted as ultimately real. They are obviously contingent and conditioned. They have a beginning in time and an end in time. They derive their existence from the fruitful combination of other existents. And their particularity or individuality is eventually dissolved into other modes of existence.

In ultimate analysis, the particular existents of the world may be said to be the offspring of the cosmic creative energy of Being. Mountains and rivers, plants and vegetables, animals and men, are formed and reformed, are born and reborn, out of the cosmic creative energy. The cosmic energy is not blind and mechanical. To be sure, it is not to be anthropomorphically conceived in the image of man's rational consciousness. Nor is it to be mechanistically conceived after the fashion of a man-made machine. There seems to be a kind of deep intuitive nonreflective intelligence operative in the creative energy of the world. It is guided in its creative functioning by intuitive apprehension of various possibilities and forms of self-expression. And therein lies the ultimate ontological foundation of the Platonic doctrine of Ideas or universals. Universals in ultimate analysis represent the infinite possibilities inherent in the structure of Being. They are reflections in human consciousness of the dynamic potentials of life and existence.

Thus we see that existence is the concrete expression of Being. Essence is the abstract potentiality of Being. Essence is not real apart from existence. Prior to actualization in existence it is a mere possibility. On the other hand, existence is meaningless apart from essence. Existence represents the actualizing of certain essences, certain potentials, of the universal life-force, plus a depth dimension of Being beyond all essences. There is no existence without some recognizable characteristics which can be defined in terms of essence or idea. But after all the characteristics of an existent have been taken note of, there is an indefinable and indeterminable dimension which remains beyond all definition. It is the depth dimension of the existing individual. This is where man's freedom lies. This is where the unfathomable mystery of Being lies. This is also the explanation of the unpredictable behavior of even a tiny electron, not to speak of a highly evolved human individual. The finest spiritual achievements of man have been due to his insight into the unfathomable mystery of Being. Awareness of the mystery of his own existence leads him to the discovery of his rootedness in the vastness of cosmic Being.

Now, it is not without significance that essences or universal forms are also called ideas. Essences are the class characteristics of different types of object and different species of living beings. For instance, the universal of tableness or tablehood is the defining essence of all those items of furniture known as tables. The universal of dogness is the defining essence of the species of animals known as dogs. The universal goodness is the defining essence of all those modes of conduct which can be considered good. Now such definable essences of different types of being are in a large measure the result of the defining activity of thought. Various essences are not distinguishable without the distinguishing activity of the rational mind. They are abstracted by reason from the flux of experience.

So the question now arises: Are not the distinct essences or universals colored by the distinguishing activity of thought? Thought is not a mere process of mirroring. It is a creative function. In distinguishing definable features of reality, it also creates them in a profound sense. Viewed from another standpoint, thought distorts and disfigures them to some degree. Nothing can remain quite the same when it is abstracted or torn out of its own original context and transferred from the concrete to the abstract. The so-called universal characteristics are one thing when submerged in the flux of experience. They become another thing when transferred from the chaotic mass of sense impressions to the rarefied region of conceptual abstraction.

It follows then that universals like tableness, dogness, goodness, etc. have a dual aspect. In one aspect they are distinguishable objective features of reality. In another aspect they are products of the distinguishing activity of thought. As contemplated by man, they are real-unreal. They are subject-object determinations. They are different modes of expression of Being as colored by thinking or knowing. They are objective features of reality, subjectively determined. If the rationalist is right in emphasizing the objective reality of Ideas, the pragmatist is right in stressing their subjective aspect and pragmatic validity. It is only in the fitness of things that as scientific knowledge expands, our concepts of tableness, dogness, goodness, etc. are substantially modified.

One very important conclusion follows from the above. We noted before that essences do not exist apart from the concrete world of changing particulars. They are real only insofar as they are ingredient in the concrete changing phenomena. Failure to understand this fact gave rise to supernaturalistic theology and dualistic metaphysics. Now we are in a position to grasp another important truth about Ideas. They are not unalterably fixed truths. They are not unchanging and unchangeable patterns of perfection. Ideas have to be reinterpreted in order to retain their pragmatic validity. With the change of social-political structure, with the alteration of the intellectual climate, our concepts of different types of being, our concepts of war and peace, of justice and injustice, of good and evil, have to be remolded.

That is why in every new age the necessity arises for reconstructing our ethical, political and religious ideas about essential truths. Our ideas of God, soul and immortality, of freedom, justice and equality, have to be recast and reinterpreted in the changing epochs of history. Every now and then the necessity arises in the history of civilization for a fresh look at our basic notions of truth, beauty, goodness, freedom, etc. Those who wish to be rigidly conservative under all circumstances, clinging to old ideas as unalterably fixed truths, betray a closed mind. They turn a blind eye to the challenge of altered situations. They close themselves tragically to new vistas of thought and new dimensions of reality.

The integral outlook reconciles idealism and pragmatism. It also reconciles essentialism and existentialism. Essences or ideas reflect the objective features of reality. But they are also subjectively colored by thought and by the changing need of the human psyche. Their value consists in their practical usefulness in different circumstances of life. Essences thus owe their reality on the one hand to the fundamental structure of the universe and on the other to the requirements of our practical life.

Human existence is not void of an essential structure. It is not shot out of a pistol. It is in the nature of "supervenient perfection" emerging upon a protracted process of evolution. Human reality cannot be understood except in terms of its organic relationship to evolutionary nature. The creativity of nature comes alive with a new organ of articulation in man. Organic relationship to nature is thus an essential characteristic of human reality. Another essential feature of human reality is man's organic relationship to society. Considered apart from his social background, he is a mere abstraction. He cannot completely fulfill himself apart from his social medium. Still another essential characteristic of man is his relationship to the realm of value. He has a growing insight into the potentialities of life, and can accordingly set before himself worthy ideals to strive for.

Man cannot fulfill himself as man by running contrary to the essential truths about himself. Freedom divorced from such essential truths is an empty and abstract form. No amount of abstract freedom asserted absolutely or solemnly proclaimed from the housetop can produce any authentic value. Nor can it bring fulfillment to the human psyche.

Let us consider the case of a person who wantonly destroys a neighbor's property for sheer fun of it or poisons his rich uncle to get his property. Such behavior may be a pure act of freedom but would not make a positive value. On the contrary it would be monstrous abuse of freedom, giving rise to a reprehensible disvalue. Such essential principles as justice, truth, love, etc. can alone provide definite content to freedom. Freedom is a value only as an unimpeded and unrestrained channel of expression of determinate higher values.

Man gradually becomes man by living in the light of his growing insight into the essential structures of his being. His existence acquires depth from his actual relationship to the realm of objective values. His freedom becomes fruitful in proportion to his concern for higher values which are objectively rooted in his relationship to the cosmic whole.

Chapter 6

THE IDEA OF THE ABSOLUTE

The idea of the Absolute is fundamental to philosophical thinking. It is the central theme of all metaphysical speculation and the nisus of inspiration to all ontological quests.

Just as matter is the key notion of physics, life is the key notion of biology, mind is the key notion of psychology, God is the key notion of religion, so also the absolute is the key notion of philosophy. For, philosophy is essentially an inquiry into the essential structure of the universe as a whole. The absolute is the universe in its wholeness. It is Being in its fullness. It is the all of existence in its allness.

The Meaning of the Absolute

"The Absolute" essentially means that which is not related to anything outside of it. Whatever is related to an external entity is finite, relative and conditioned. The Absolute is infinite, all-comprehensive and unconditioned.

In its positive essence, the absolute is the cosmic whole. The cosmic whole is not related to anything external, for the simple reason that there is nothing external to it. It is the totality of all that is. It is the ultimate ground of all being. It is the all-encompassing medium of existence in which all things and creatures live, move and have their being. Out of which everything arises, and into which everything is dissolved again.

As all-comprehensive, the Absolute is essentially non-dual. It embraces the one as well as the many. Therefore, it cannot be identified with either the one or the many.

Some philosophers interpret the universe pluralistically, whereas some interpret it monistically. But both pluralism and monism presuppose the notion of the Absolute as the cosmic whole. Both pluralism and monism are affirmed as absolutely true versions of the universe as a whole. They are put forward as final truths about the absolute.

For instance, both Bertrand Russell and William James affirm a pluralistic universe. They reject the notion of any universal creative principle. But both are trying to say something about the universe as a whole. For Russell the universe in its primordial essence is the sum total of sense-data which are neither material nor mental. Material and mental phenomena are different modes of configuration of neutral sense data. Even when material and mental phenomena are differentiated, they do not cease to be sense data arranged and rearranged in various ways.

Similarly, William James describes the primordial stuff of existence as the flux of pure experience. All manner of sensations and relations intermingle in the structure of pure experience such as the "big booming buzzing confusion" of the infant's mind. With the growth of intellectual faculties, different types of sensation and relation are gradually distinguished. Mind and matter are different modes of configuration of the multitudinous items of pure experience. As among the items of experience there exist all manner of relations such as conjunctions and disjunctions, harmonies and discords, attractions and repulsions. Which means that the world in which we live is not an unchanging symmetrical block universe, but a pluralistic scheme of dynamic flux.

But, be it noted here, that a pluralistic scheme is still asserted to be an absolute truth about the universe as a whole. Had pluralism been an affirmation of truth about only a portion of the universe, it would have been only a partial truth, subject to radical transformation in the wider context of the whole. Pluralism denies the oneness of the universe. But it is still concerned with the wholeness of the universe. It repudiates the substantive character and the centralized structure of the Absolute. But nonetheless it itself employs the notion of the Absolute. If further light can be obtained regarding the structure of the Absolute via experiences other than sensuous observation and scientific thinking, pluralism can have no reasonable objection to that. That is why we find that in his *Varieties of Religious Experience*, William James, by virtue of his sterling quality of open-mindedness, seems willing to accept a nontemporal dimension of reality transcending both unity and plurality, conjunction and disjunction. The reality of such a nontemporal dimension of Being seems to be the unequivocal testimony of the profoundest religious experiences of mankind.

Now, in contrast with pluralism, monism offers a monistic interpretation of the cosmic whole. It identifies the whole as one universal creative principle. It proceeds to derive the plurality of phenomena from that principle of creative unity. From the standpoint of pure intellect, it is extremely difficult to decide whether the monistic interpretation is true or not. It may be true. But again it may not be true. In the absence of verification in terms of universal experience, monism is, logically speaking, a mere hypothesis. It has a great emotional appeal. It has a good deal of religious importance. But it is necessarily a big question mark in rational thinking.

In any event, let us repeat, even when monism is rejected as a cosmological theory, that does not amount to a rejection of the idea of the Absolute. We have seen that pluralism presupposes the notion of the absolute no less than monism. Only, monism adds something more to the notion of the absolute. It adds the concept of the One as creator of the Many. It identifies the Absolute as the One. Such an identification may perhaps be vindicated on the basis of religious and mystical experience. But it is also possible that the monistic conception of the absolute as the One is only an "Idea of Reason," to use an expression of Immanuel Kant. It may be just a speculative ideal, an heuristic maxim for our intellectual operations, but not an objective reality. On intellectual grounds, one can never be quite sure of the truth of the monistic hypothesis.

But regardless of the truth or falsity of the monistic hypothesis, the concept of the absolute stands. It is the all-comprehensive existence-total. Phenomenologically, this total is the unity of all phenomena. Theistically interpreted, it is God, the creator of all phenomena. Pantheistically, it is the underlying spiritual substance and ground of all phenomena.

The idea of the Absolute is to be found in scientific thinking as well as in mystical testimony. Science envisages the Absolute as the vast space-time continuum within which worlds without number are formed, broken and reformed. Or, the Absolute may be posited as that unified field of energy within which gravitational as well as electromagnetic phenomena are controlled by some ultimate uniform laws.

Mystical experience reveals the absolute as the one all-encompassing ocean of consciousness. Or, it may even go deeper and posit the absolute as the boundless void, the nameless nondual, which gives birth to the conscious as well as the unconscious, to the real as well as the unreal.

Integral philosophy reconciles science and mysticism. It conceives of the absolute as the dynamic Being, of which the space-time continuum is the medium of self-expression. It is the unified field of energy, which is nontemporal in its depth dimension. It is the limitless matrix, out of which the material and the spiritual evolve as closely interrelated processes. Also emerge from it in the course of evolution such gradations of its self-manifestation as the unconscious, the conscious and the superconscious.

Now, inherent in the structure of the absolute or the universe as a whole there are some interrelated forces. A creative urge, a sustaining power, and a destructive impulse coexist within the absolute. The Hindu trinity of Brahmā, Viṣṇu and Rudra is a religious way of representing these interrelated forces in the structure of Being. Phenomenologically speaking, these concepts are descriptive of such obvious and introvertible processes of life as birth, growth and death, creation, survival and destruction. A philosopher is under no obligation to visualize such processes as activities of one infinite substance or first cause such as God. The idea of God as one universal creative Mind is bound to remain always a mere article of faith and an unverifiable hypothesis. But it is part of the task of philosophy to make it clear that creation, existence, and destruction are intertwined processes inherent in the structure of reality. They are processes continuously going on within the comprehensive unity of the cosmic whole. This is a fundamental truth about reality which is beyond all doubt and dispute.

It is evident from the above that the Absolute is non-dual (*advaita*) in more than one sense. It is nondual insofar as it embraces both conjunctions and disjunctions, harmonies and discords, unities and pluralities, as indubitable facts of experience. It is also nondual insofar as it embraces both physical and psychical phenomena, matter and mind, nature and spirit, unconscious and conscious, as interrelated processes of our experience-continuum. Furthermore, it is nondual insofar as it embraces both creation and destruction, birth and death, as interrelated processes in the cosmic flow.

Having clarified the meaning of the Absolute as the key concept of philosophy, we are now in a position to undertake a brief survey of some of the representative theories regarding the distinctive character of the absolute.

The Absolute has indeed been conceived in widely divergent ways. Consequent upon wide differences of approach, we have the physical absolute, the vital absolute, the mental absolute, and the mystical or spiritual absolute. According to the integral viewpoint, different theories of the Absolute are different perspectives of the same multidimensional Being. They are different modes of interpretation of the essence of ultimate reality. But like blind men's conflicting versions of the same elephant, they represent partial and fragmentary truths regarding sundered aspects of the same Being.

The Physical Absolute (Annam Brahman)

Materialism is inspired by the notion of the physical Absolute. In its view, the universe in its primordial essence is matter. Matter is the ground of all existence. All things including plants, animals and men are born out of matter, sustained by matter, and dissolved again into matter. Matter contains, as Tyndall says, "the promise and potency of the whole of terrestrial life."

Now, what is matter? Descartes defined it as that absolutely unconscious substance which is the polar opposite of mind. So the physical absolute may be conceived as the one infinite unconscious substance which gives rise to all the things and beings of the world. Or, it may be conceived as an infinity of further irreducible, unconscious particles of substance called atoms. Some believe that these atoms, each self-existent and self-contained, were originally whirling through infinite space, jostling with one another, combining and re-combining to form all manner of complex structures.

Today, the notion of material substance as the unchanging and unchangeable substratum of physical phenomena has been rejected as a trans-empirical concept. We always perceive change. The unchanging is an illusion of intellect. We always perceive phenomena. Any mysterious substance behind phenomena is an unnecessary hypothesis.

Modern physics has also established that electrons which are essential components of atoms, are no more particles than waves. They behave sometimes like waves and sometimes like particles. However contradictory it may sound, they are "wavicles", i.e., both waves and particles. Which suggests that the whole conception of electron is only a mental picture of some unknown force which is unpredictable in behavior.

In modern science, the former dualism of mass and motion has been resolved into the monistic conception of energy. In his Special Theory of Relativity, Albert Einstein demonstrates the equivalence of matter and energy. While motion is kinetic energy, mass is potential energy. The energy that slumbers in mass can be released. But are there not radically different types of energy? On the one hand, there are gravitational forces. On the other, there are such electromagnetic forces as light, heat, X-rays, radio-waves, gamma rays, etc. Gravitational phenomena are reduced by Einstein to a geometrical property of the space-time continuum. But electro-magnetic phenomena are explained by Max Planck in terms of the concept of energy-quanta, i.e., discrete units of energy. Thus there seems to exist an abysmal gulf between the gravitational phenomena of outer space and the electromagnetic phenomena of atomic energy.

In his Unified Field Theory, which is the final triumph of Einstein's creative genius, he bridges the gulf. He catches a glimpse of the unified structure of the universe. He shows how gravitational and electromagnetical phenomena are inseparably related to each other. They are unified within one basic superstructure of universal law. They are interrelated modes of manifestation of one all-encompassing energy-field.

Another interesting form in which the physical Absolute has been conceived in recent times is that of Space-Time. Professor S. Alexander has conceived of Space-Time as one infinite and continuous whole, of which Space may be metaphorically described as the body, and Time as the mind.[1] Space and time are not to be regarded as the forms of any ontologically prior substance such as matter. Space-Time itself is the most fundamental stuff of which all things, whether as substances or as phenomena are made.[2] It is envisaged as one all-encompassing system

[1] S. Alexander, *Space, Time and Deity,* Vol. II (London: Macmillan & Co., 1934), p. 38.

[2] Alexander, op. cit., Vol. I (London: Macmillan & Co., 1927), p. 341.

of motion within which different empirical existents are differentiated as different complexes of motion. Material objects, plants and vegetables, different species of animals, human beings, etc. form a graded hierarchy of qualitative differences emerging from the evolutionary movement of Space-Time. Space-Time is essentially impregnated with a creative nisus. Evolution is the outcome of the creative urge inherent in Space-Time. Matter, life, mind, spirit, etc. are the emergent offspring of that creative urge.

The Vital Absolute (Prāṇa Brahman)

Vitalism is inspired by the concept of the Absolute as one universal life-force. Henri Bergson is a forceful exponent of the vitalistic position. In his view, the universe in its primordial form is not matter, but life. Not physical energy but vital impulse, the *élan vital*. Static matter is an illusion of intellect. The intellect, which is a tool of our practical life needs static positions from which to move. It needs halting stations where to rest in the course of life's movement. And it also needs satisfactory destinations for which to strive. So by virtue of its built-in cinematographic mechanism it takes immobile snapshots of the mobility of the real. Matter represents these static snapshots. No wonder then that intellect should be perfectly at home in the realm of matter. But it misses the living mobility of ultimate reality.

Whereas Alexander starts with Space-Time, Bergson starts with Time. Time is the absolutely free principle of creativity. In its creation of ever new forms and qualities, it is not determined either mechanistically or teleologically. Life is the spontaneous creativity of time. Space is only the trajectory of time's free movement. It is the external appearance of the mobility of time.

Reality then is time, change, movement. Life represents the forward movement of reality making itself. Matter represents the backward movement of reality already made and then unmaking itself. Let us say reality is like a fireworks display. Matter would then be like "black cinders of the spent rockets that are falling dead".[3] Life would then be the upward movement of fresh rockets blazing a fiery path across those black cinders.

Life is an unconscious principle of creativity. Mind, spirit, etc. progressively evolve in the course of the creative process. The highest spiritual ideal consists in active co-operation with the creative force of evolution. The meaning of God is to be found in the creativity of the "original impetus of life".[4]

The Mental Absolute (Manas Brahman)

Much of religious idealism is inspired by the concept of the Absolute as one universal mind, called God. Mind with its superior attribute of consciousness is a richer category. The attempt therefore to derive mind from either matter or life amounts to producing something out of nothing. It is a violation of the fundamental maxim of thought: Ex nihilo nihil fit.

Both materialism and vitalism, according to religious idealism, commit the fallacy of hysteron proteron, i.e., putting the cart before the horse. The concepts of both matter and life, as we understand them, presuppose the reality of the understanding mind. Perception and understanding make them what they are. In other words, they presuppose the mind of which perception and understanding are essential functions. Not the mind of any particular human being, but the universal mind which functions through different finite spirits.

So it is the universal mind, that is God, to which both matter and life owe their existence. The universal mind includes in its connotation being plus energy plus intelligence. So matter and life can be derived from it. But neither matter nor life, none of which is endowed with intelligence, can possibly create the intelligent mind.

---

[3] Henri Bergson, Arthur Mitchell trans., Creative Evolution, p. 264.
[4] Ibid., p. 92.

Now, the universal mind is usually conceived in dualistic terms, because mind is essentially dualistic in thinking. Religion posits the universal mind as the mind of a sovereign Being known as God, who is extracosmic and transcendent in character. The world of nature and man, created by God, is believed to exist outside of Him as the object of His paternal care.

But the notion of an extracosmic universal mind is for obvious reasons philosophically untenable. The sovereign mind, insofar as it is over and above the imperfect world, is limited by the external existence of the world. So, for all its sovereign power it ceases to be the absolute. Moreover, by reason of its existence in space outside of the world of matter, it ceases to be spiritual in the strict sense of the term.

The Absolute as Supermind (Vijñānam Brahman)

Spiritual nondualism is inspired by the concept of the Absolute as supermind. The supermind is the sovereign dynamism of ultimate reality. It is the creative light of Being. It is the all-embracing consciousness, nondualistic in structure.

The supermind originates and unifies both matter and mind, even though it is radically different from both in character and mode of operation. In ultimate analysis, neither mind is derived from matter, nor matter is derived from mind. Matter and mind are relative to each other. They presuppose each other. They are involved in each other. If matter is the physical support for mental operations, mind is the organizing principle in the organization of matter. Both of them owe their existence to a higher creative principle. They are different grades of manifestation of Being through the creativity of the supermind.

The supermind embraces and unifies both the conscious and the unconscious. Rational consciousness cannot be derived solely from unconscious mentality. Nor can the unconscious mind be explained as a kind of rational intelligence which has "collapsed into immediacy." The unconscious and the conscious are different grades of manifestation of Being through the creativity of the supermind. In the course of evolution, that is, the progressive self-manifestation of Being, the unconscious, the conscious and the superconscious appear as more and more luminous reflections within the evolving organism of the self-light of Being.

The supermind transcends and yet unifies the one and the many. The one and the many interpenetrate in the concrete texture of the universe. Being is to be identified neither with the one nor with the many. It is an infinitely rich principle of unity-in-plurality and plurality-in-unity. The manifoldness of the world cannot be reduced to a mere illusion of perception. Nor can the unity of existence be reduced to a mere illusion of intellect. In the organismic structure of the world there is an all-pervasive presence of each in all and all in each. The uniqueness of existing individual things and beings is no less an important aspect of life than their impregnable togetherness in the cosmic whole.

The supermind does not exist over and above the world. It embraces the entire universe within its comprehensive unity. There is no ontological gulf separating the universe from the supermind. The universe of countless solar systems and galaxies exists like a string of islands within the limitless ocean of Being of which the supermind is the dynamic self-luminosity.

The Absolute as Spirit (Ānandam Brahman)

A single ray from the supermind can afford us a glimpse of the Absolute as spirit. This means that such a spiritual values as truth, beauty and goodness, love, joy and freedom, are objectively rooted in the structure of Being. They are not merely elements of man's wishful thinking. They are the secret driving forces in the process of cosmic evolution. They are the values that set the direction in which the world is moving. They represent the hidden potentialities of life. The supreme reality is the unity of such values.

All intrinsic values can be summed up in the concept of bliss (*ānanda*). Bliss is the experience of such absolute values as truth, beauty, justice, love, freedom, etc. It is the practice of such values. It is the actual fulfillment of such values. Bliss is pure existence. To exist is to experience joy. And to experience joy is to continue to exist. Bliss is also pure consciousness. To exist is to be aware— to be aware of things as they are. And to be aware of things as they are is the glory of existence.

So the Absolute is now revealed as pure existence, pure consciousness, and pure joy. It is the indivisible unity of these absolute values. It is Saccidānanda, i.e., existence-knowledge-bliss. In a very important sense, existence and knowledge are attributes of bliss. As the Upaniṣad says,[5] the world with its endless variations springs into existence out of the fullness of joy. All existing things abide in joy. They are also fulfilled in joy. So the absolute is the fullness of joy. It is that fullness of joy which sustains every creature in his self-existence, inspires him in his self-expression, and completes him in his self-fulfilment.

The Absolute as Indeterminable Being (*Nirguṇa Brahman*)

Having perceived the significance of Spirit (Saccidānanda) as a key to the understanding of the absolute, critical intelligence is likely to discover that even Spirit is not the last word. Consciousness and bliss, or love, joy, beauty, truth, etc. are, after all, human experiences. They are in the last analysis, anthropomorphic notions. In characterizing the absolute in terms of such notions, the human mind does indeed reach the highest limit of its ability to fathom the mystery of Being. But the absolute is higher

---

[5] *Taittirīya Upaniṣad*, III. 6. 1.

than the highest (parātpara). It cannot be equated with anthropomorphic notions or with any construction of the human intellect. Such notions do certainly afford us a profound insight into the structure of Being. But they can hardly be said to exhaust the mystery of Being. That is why when an authentic mystic is truly admitted into the mystery of Being, transcending the furthest boundaries of the human mind, he becomes speechless. He finds his experience to be absolutely incommunicable. He realizes the supreme truth as the great Silence (Śāntam Brahman).

So the great Buddha characterized the ultimate mystery of Being as Emptiness (Śūnyatā). Śankara characterized it as Formlessness (Nirguṇatā). Meister Eckhart describes it as "the absolute nudity of pure Being". Berdyaev calls it "the ineffable Nothingness".[6]

A direct encounter with the ultimate mystery of Being introduces a spiritual seeker to the pure nontemporal dimension of existence. He beholds that aspect of Being which Sri Aurobindo designates as supracosmic Transcendence.[7] From the standpoint of that transcendental experience, the world of space-time appears at the beginning as a realm of shadows. Or it may appear as valueless impermanence (tuccha), or as objective unreality (bhāvarūpa mithyā).

When the splendor of mystic illumination hits the eye of the soul, one is much too dazzled for a while to see the world any more. After a while when the world is seen again, it appears for some time as an objective unreality, as an illusory shadow-show. It takes a good deal of time for the dazzling light of mystic experience to be fully integrated into the maturing personality. It requires indeed the maturity of complete self-integration to appreciate fully the reality and intrinsic value of the world— the world of space, time and manifold individuality—as a field of ever new creation and value-emergence.

---

[6] Nicolas Berdyaev, *The Beginning and the End* (New York: Harper Torchbooks, 1957), p. 107.

[7] Sri Aurobindo, *The Life Divine*, p. 48.

Until the complete integration of personality is attained, the true spirit of creative fellowship with the Supreme cannot develop. On the contrary, a mystic might be inclined to maintain an attitude of indifference to the world, or an attitude of pity and condescension. The attitude of indifference holds forth the ideals of stoicism, asceticism, and monasticism as the most exalted modes of spiritual living. The attitude of pity prompts a career of patronizing social service imbued with the idea of the utter vanity, worthlessness or unreality of the world, or the abysmal sinfulness of life. Both of these attitudes of indifference and pity are rooted in a world-and-life-negating outlook. They stem from excessive pre-occupation with the exclusive reality of the eternal. They betray a lack of understanding of the ontological significance of time. So long as the reality of Nature and the glory of life are not fully appreciated, so long as the dynamic presence of the eternal in time is not adequately grasped, there can hardly be any full participation in life and society with a view to transforming this very world—the natural world of war and peace, of hatred and love—into a better image of the absolute.

Chapter 7

THE INTEGRAL VIEW OF THE ABSOLUTE

Integral nondualism is based upon the concept of the Absolute as fullness (pūrnam), as multidimensional Being, as the integral whole.

The Absolute as the integral whole comprises the natural, the supernatural, and the eternal.

Naturalism affirms the world of matter, life and mind as the Absolute. It rejects the notion of the supernatural. It rejects also the reality of the eternal. It considers the objective world of perceptive experience, the natural order of processes and events, as the one absolute reality.

Supernaturalism is animated by a glimpse of the eternal. But it misconstrues the eternal and, in consequence, makes two grievous mistakes. First, it drives the wedge of ontological dualism between the natural and the supernatural orders. It violates the indivisibility of Being. The truth is that both Nature (aparā prakṛti) and Supernature (parā prakṛti) are closely interrelated and inter-penetrating modes of manifestation of the same Being. Nature is the materialized form of expression of Supernature. And Supernature is the subtler mode of operation of Nature. Both Nature and Supernature are intertwined modes of operation of the same creative energy (śakti) of Being.

Secondly, supernaturalism often makes the mistake of equating the eternal with the supernatural. It thus fails to grasp the inmost essence of the eternal as the timeless dimension of existence. The supernatural is an exalted mode of existence *in time*. It is imagined as an extension of existence—a kind of etherealized and idealized existence —beyond the grave. But however etherealized, protracted

and beatified, it is nonetheless in time and therefore termi-
nable in time. That is why, according to Vedānta, existence in heaven is believed to terminate as soon as one's
religious merit is exhausted through enjoyment. Existence in heaven (swarga) is, therefore, not the ultimate
goal, but only a passing phase of one's evolution toward
the ultimate goal, namely union with the true eternal
(mokśa). The eternal can be realized here and now in
this very natural order. For, that which is essentially timeless pervades all the moments of time. It is not an attribute of the future. It is eternal now.

Exclusive mysticism goes to the other extreme, and ex-
cludes from ultimate reality both the natural and the
supernatural. It overstresses the reality of the eternal to
the extent of de-realizing the space-time continuum. It
overemphasizes the spiritual to the extent of denouncing
the value and reality of the material. It glorifies mystic
experience to the extent of undermining the will to live
and the impulse to participate in the creative adventure
of life.

The Absolute as Multidimensional Being

The truth is that Being is multidimensional. The Absolute is multidimensional Being. The natural, the supernatural, and the eternal, are different dimensions of the
same indivisible Being. The eternal is not the negation
of time. It contains within itself the creativity of time.
The world-process is time in its creative flow. The natural
and the supernatural are different modes of manifestation
of time's creative urge.

In its inmost essence Being is indeed indeterminable
(Nirguṇa). For, whatever is determinate including the
Deity is a Being, not Being as such. But the term "indeterminable" is not to be understood negatively as an
incapacity to produce determinations.[1] On the contrary,
it has to be comprehended positively as the boundless

---

[1] Sri Aurobindo, *The Life Divine*, p. 376.

and inexhaustible energy in endless varieties of determinate modes of existence, and yet remain full and infinite (pūrnam). That which is truly indeterminable is in its positive essence the creative source of endless determinations. That which is truly formless is, in its positive essence, the inexhaustible source of limitless forms. Indeterminable Being is indeed one with infinite energy. Śiva is one with Śakti. Śakti is not an attribute of Śiva, nor is Śiva an appendage to Śakti. Śiva and Śakti, existence and energy, are two inseparable aspects of the same Being. Just as the existence of fire and the burning capacity of fire are one and the same thing.

The Absolute as the Psycho-Cosmic Continuum

The Absolute is the integral whole not only in the sense that it is the totality of all objective phenomena. The objective total, the cosmic panorama, is only one aspect of Being. It is relative to the subject which knows, just as the subject is relative to the object which is known. The cosmic order is as much relative to the psyche,—to the ordering and unifying power of the psyche—as the psyche is relative to the cosmos—to the function of the cosmos as its sustaining medium. Subject and object interpenetrate in the structure of Being. The Absolute is, therefore, to use a term of Karl Jaspers,[2] "the Comprehensive," in which the dichotomy of subject and object is dissolved. It is the psychocosmic continuum from which psyche and cosmos, for all their differentiation, cannot break away.

In a full understanding of the absolute, affirmation has to be followed by negation, and negation again must be followed by deeper affirmation. In one's search for the absolute, one has first of all to push beyond the barriers of superficial observation and isolating imagination. Rigorously following the path of negation, one has to reject the claims of matter, life, mind, etc. to be the absolute.

---

[2] Karl Jaspers, *Way to Wisdom* (New Haven: Yale University Press, 1954), p. 30.

They represent delimited or abstracted areas of experience. They signify fragmentary aspects of Being. So, none of them can be exalted to the rank of the Absolute. The Absolute in its essential structure must transcend all determinate modes of existence in order to creatively embrace them all.

But having gained an insight into the pure and transcendent essence of Being, our attention has once more to be directed to the concrete fullness of Being. Within the framework of our comprehensive truth-vision, matter, life, mind, etc. have again to be affirmed, not in their superficial appearance, but in their essential structure. They would now fall into their right place as the richly diversified content of Being. They would now be understood as inter-related factors in the creativity of Being.

Being in its inmost essence is not matter, not life, not mind, not reason, etc. But from that the conclusion is not to be drawn that any of them is unreal. Negatives must be supplemented by affirmatives. Superficial affirmation needs to be corrected by negation. But that negation must again be negated in total and integrated affirmation. The essence of wisdom lies in one's ability to say that Being is matter, Being is life, Being is mind, Being is reason, etc. without committing the fallacy of false equation. The true Absolute "takes all relativities in its embrace."[3] It is because the absolute is nothing in particular that it can produce everything in its full glory.

The Absolute as the Ground of all Existence and Value

When the word existence is used to mean the finite and contingent existence of an individual, the Absolute is beyond both existence and nonexistence. Both existing things and non-existing facts and ideas are embraced within the unity of the Absolute. But there is a sense in which the Absolute may be characterized as infinite existence,

---

[3] Sri Aurobindo, *The Life Divine*, p. 384.

provided that sense is carefully noted. It is infinite exist-ence not in the sense that it is an infinite self-existent substance. That would be an intellectual construction resulting from the application of the human category of substance-quality. That would be an interpretation of Being, and not Being as such. Nor can the Absolute be said to be infinite existence in the sense that existence is an immutable Platonic Idea that shines in a heavenly abode. Existence is no Idea or complex of Ideas. As the ground of all Ideas, it has ontological priority over them. Ideas are mere abstractions of thought apart from exist-ence. They are real only as possibilities inherent in the structure of Being. They become valid only by virtue of "ingression"[4] in actual phenomena.

The Absolute can be said to be infinite existence only in the sense that it is the ground of all existing things which emerge from it and again get dissolved in it. Truly speaking, the Absolute is no existent, not even an infinite existent, but the source and ground of all existence.

It is in the same way that we have to understand the meaning of infinite consciousness, infinite love, etc. The absolute is not an infinite substance endowed with the attribute of consciousness. That would make the Absolute a product of human categorizing or rational interpreta-tion. All conscious substances are related to consciousness in the same way that all material objects are related to space. Material objects are in essence particular configura-tions of events which are differentiated within the matrix of one infinite space or energy-field. Likewise, conscious substances are particular configurations of events which are differentiated within the matrix of one infinite and undivided consciousness (nirvibhāga citi) or existence-field.

Nor can the Absolute be said to be infinite consciousness in the sense that it is an immutable Platonic Idea or Es-sence of consciousness shining in an eternal abode. The Idea of consciousness is an abstraction of thought, whereas

---

[4] Alfred North Whitehead, *Process and Reality* (New York: Harper & Brothers, Harper Torchbooks, 1960), p. 34.

consciousness is the presupposition of all thinking. The Essence of consciousness is an object of reason, whereas consciousness is the prius of all reasoning. The Idea or Essence of consciousness is real only as a possibility inherent in the structure of Being. Whenever suitable empirical conditions arise, Being is manifested in the form of a conscious being, a spiritual entity. So, the Absolute can be said to be infinite consciousness only in the sense that it is the ground of all conscious being. As creatures evolve in respect of their inward refinement and receptivity to the glory of Being, they become more and more conscious.

Similarly, the Absolute is not infinite love in the sense that it is an infinite substance endowed with universal love. That would de-absolutize the Absolute, reducing it to "an each among eaches," a Primus inter pares. Hateful creatures would fall outside of the life of the absolute. We shall be back to the deistic conception of a Loving Deity presiding over sinful creatures who take delight more in hatred than in love. Moreover, by virtue of our wishful thinking the Absolute would be transformed into an anthropomorphic Being, fashioned after the image of man.

The Absolute cannot also be said to be infinite love in the sense that it is the Idea or Essence of universal love. The Idea of love is a mere abstraction of thought apart from actual love relations. It is real only as a possibility inherent in the structure of Being.

The Absolute can be characterized as infinite love only in the sense that it is the ground and source of all love relations. Whenever a person acts, thinks and lives in harmony with the structure of Being, he experiences love in his heart. And in the depth of his love he experiences the Absolute. On the contrary, whenever a person lives out of tune with the structure of Being, or in violation of his relationship with the Absolute, he experiences hatred. And in hatred he experiences his alienation from Being, from the ground of his own existence.

Truth, Beauty, and Goodness

The Absolute is the ultimate ground of all such values as truth, beauty and goodness. They are relational, not intrinsic characteristics of the Absolute. Truth is the Absolute insofar as it is known or unveiled. Beauty is the Absolute insofar as it is felt or immediately perceived in sense-impressions. Goodness is the Absolute insofar as it is expressed in integrated actions. In other words, the Absolute is truth as the harmony of thoughts and ideas. The Absolute is beauty as the harmony of feelings and sensations. The Absolute is goodness as the harmony of desires and actions.

Let us further clarify the matter with specific reference to truth. What will be found to be true with regard to truth will also apply to the other values.

Truth is the absolute *qua* known or revealed to the mind. It is, therefore, to use a suggestive phrase of Professor Alexander,[5] "a subject-object determination." It is the value that emerges from the mind's contact with the Absolute. Now, the mind's contact with the Absolute, is knowledge—very essential knowledge. Truth is therefore the object of knowledge.

But human knowledge is always by its very nature relative. It is what the knowing mind gains by contemplating Being under certain circumstances from a certain standpoint. In thus contemplating Being it is always a particular aspect, characteristic, or dimension of Being which is revealed at a given time. Truth as an object of knowledge is, therefore, always a definite perspective of Being. It can hardly be absolutely equated with the Absolute. In transcending the knower-known distinction, the absolute transcends truth. That is why Kena Upaniṣad says: "If thou thinkest that thou knowest It well, little indeed dost thou know the form of the Brahman."[6] But yet the

---

[5] S. Alexander, *Space, Time and Deity,* Vol. II, p. 238.

[6] Sri Aurobindo, *Kena Upaniṣad* (Pondicherry: Sri Aurobindo Ashram, 1952), p. 5.

Absolute is not unknown and unknowable, as agnosticism would have us believe. Because the Absolute is increasingly unveiled in respect of its various aspects in the gradual expansion of our knowledge. In its essence, the Absolute is immediately encountered in our intuitive realization or nondualistic experience. The Absolute is not to be identified with any object of knowledge. But it is the all-inclusive basis of the knower-known distinction. It is the ground of all knowledge. It is the ground of all true judgments and propositions. When a person makes a statement in which some aspect of Being is revealed, his statement is true to that extent. If his statement is out of tune with the intended aspect of Being, it is false.

Now, we are in a position to say that truth is a mode of manifestation of the Absolute. It is identical with the Absolute in the sense that it is the Absolute as unveiled. It is different from the Absolute on the ground that whereas it is a definite object of knowledge, the Absolute which is in essence indeterminable transcends the subject-object polarization.

What unmistakably follows from the above is that all humanly known truth is essentially relative. All humanly known religious dogmas, philosophical doctrines, and political ideologies are only relatively true. They are valid and useful under certain circumstances and for certain purposes. But none of them can be absolutely valid for all times and for all peoples. An unconscious identification of any definitely formulated truth with the absolute is the prolific source of dogmatism, fanaticism, ideological aggressiveness, and holy crusades.

A clear understanding of the relativity of all humanly known truths is an essential condition of abiding world peace. And of humble and harmonious co-operation among the different religious and political groups of the world in the best interests of the progress of civilization.

Chapter 8

CHANGE AND PERMANENCE

Recognition of the reality of change and the significance of evolution is the most distinctive feature of modern thought. Time is acknowledged today as an ultimate category. It is not only an image of eternity. It is a component of ultimate reality.

There can be no denying the fact that the world is always astir with movement. It is indeed a perpetual flux and flow. Change is the "stuff" of which the world is made. It is above everything else a spatial-temporal scheme. The Sanskrit word for the world is (*Jagat*), which means that it is always on the go, whithersoever it may be going. The perpetually changing and moving nature of the world is brought out into relief in such analogies as the running stream, the burning flame, the flying bird, etc.

Heraclitus says that the world is like a flowing river in which a man cannot take his bath twice. When he gets down into a river to take his bath for the second time, he is sure to find it a different river, because the waters in which he had his first bath must have flowed far away during the interval. A disciple of Heraclitus remarks that a person cannot bathe even once in the same river. Standing on the bank of the river he concentrates on a mass of water where he is going to have a dip. By the time he reaches there it has gone far away and is replaced by another moving mass of water.

The Hindu-Buddhist tradition has laid much stress upon the impermanence of the world. Nothing lasts long here. Everything is ephemeral, evanescent, transitory. Not a moment passes without leaving its marks upon phenomena. Time bites into everything, penetrates it, and sweeps it along in a process of continuous change. The world is indeed an ever-changing fast-moving process, not a finished product.

Now, what is the precise significance of the perpetual change characteristic of the world? Is change ultimately real? If not, how far, or in what sense can it be said to be real? The metaphysical inquiry about change concerns its ontological status or mode of existence from the ultimate standpoint, and its mode of connection with the ultimate philosophical principle.

Theories of Change as Illusory

A widespread belief of ancient times is that that which changes is *ipso facto* unreal. Permanence or stability is affirmed to be the very essence of reality. The real is that which abides, which defies all changes and scoffs at all mutations. Consequently, change is another name for nonbeing; it is a process of losing and gaining, which is an evident mark of imperfection. As immutable being, the real is eternal perfection; it has no excellence to gain, and no deficiency to cast out. Change or becoming is not only a mark of imperfection, but is also believed to be incomprehensible to thought. Zeno, the great dialectician of ancient Greece, points out that the alleged change or movement of a thing, when it is submitted to critical examination, discloses fatal self-contradictions within it. The dialectic of thought resolves it into a string of paradoxes. This emboldens his renowned successor Parmenides to declare that Being—unchanging and unchangeable Being—is the only reality, and that becoming is a mere illusion. Zeno's destructive criticism of the concept of Becoming prepares the ground for Parmenides' emphatic affirmation of Being as the sole ultimate reality.

The above view is believed to be further reinforced by the following consideration. Had Reality been subject to change, it would have to become either more or less than itself, whether in respect of quantity or in respect of quality. But reality cannot become more than itself, because that would be flagrant violation of the fundamental maxim of thought, "Nothing comes out of nothing" (*ex nihilo nihil fit*). Reality cannot also become less than itself, because that would involve the notion of total annihilation of some portion of reality. The conception of total annihilation is no less absurd and inconsistent than the conception of absolute creation out of nothing.

Furthermore, according to rationalists, reality is inseparable from knowledge. It is essentially rational, intelligible, or knowable. Had reality been constantly changing, it would have been simply incapable of being known. No sooner we grasp a thing than it becomes something other than itself. What we succeed in knowing is always the dead past of a continuous process of change. So, Plato concludes that reality must be a fixed system of eternal and unchangeable Forms or Ideas. The world of becoming is only a realm of shadows, and it is perpetually torn between being and nonbeing.

The Śaṅkarite School of Indian Philosophy does not reduce change, as does Parmenides, to a pure illusion of the senses. The changing world of phenomena represents in its view a particular type, order or level of reality. It enjoys what has been called empirical, conventional, or pragmatic type of reality (*vyavahāric sattvā*). It is real from the standpoint of primal ignorance (*māyā* or *avidyā*). It is not a mere function of the senses, nor a subjective modification of the percipient mind. It is a product of the creative activity of the cosmic principle of nescience (*māyā*) and is therefore presented as an independent datum to the mind that perceives it. But as a creation of nescience, the world of change stands condemned as a positive falsehood (*bhāvarūpamithyā*) as soon as the temporal point of view is transcended and replaced by the nontemporal standpoint of ultimate reality. This view amounts, not to a categorical denial of change as an empty nothing, but to the affirmation of the world of change as a real-unreal sort of reality, an indescribable mystery. While it is real from one standpoint, it is unreal from another. Real from the standpoint of ignorance, it is unreal from the standpoint of supreme knowledge.

Theories of Change as a Subordinate Element of Reality

The above view of the world of change as an objective falsehood is quite naturally unacceptable to the rationalistic way of thinking. Hegelian philosophers, for instance, prefer to look upon reality as a principle of permanence-in-change, not a principle of permanence beyond change. The world of change is, in Hegel's view, organically related to the eternally perfect Real. The eternal embraces the endless time-order, and yet transcends it. The bewildering variety of changes that characterize the temporal flux constitute the wealth of manifestation of the eternal perfection. Change is an essential factor in that which is permanent, not an eternally cancelled falsehood. Change and permanence are in truth inseparable aspects of the one concrete reality.

Be it, however, noted here that although change is an essential aspect of Reality, it is, after all, conceived as a subordinate feature of that reality. The essential and fundamental structure of Reality is ever unaffected by the ceaseless flux of change or becoming. Moreover, there is an element of the inexpressible or inexhaustible in the nature of the principle of permanence. It defies exhaustive expression in terms of change and time. It is believed that a clue to the understanding of such an unchanging principle behind change is provided by our own self-consciousness. We are constantly changing along with the changes around us; we are moving with the movement of the universe. But when we arise to an awareness of this all-pervasive change and make a survey of the stream of becoming, we are assuredly lifted into a point of view which is that of the eternal. By virtue of our self-consciousness, we seem to participate in the nature of that which embraces the flux of existence, and yet transcends it.

British Neo-Hegelians like Green and Caird have elaborated this view with great force and lucidity. The American Neo-Hegelian Josiah Royce lays emphasis upon the character of the infinite stream of becoming as a *totum simul* present at a stroke to the Absolute.[1] It is supposed to fall with all its endlessness within the infinite span of consciousness, the eternal presence, of the Supreme Spirit. In support of this view, Royce has invoked the modern psychological theory of the "specious present" and the modern mathematical theory of the infinite as a self-representative system.

The Italian neo-idealist, Gentile, also considers the temporal as an objective factor in the reality of the non-temporal. He speaks of the "resolution of the temporal into eternal history", and maintains that the "eternal is time itself considered in the actuality of mind".[2] The march of humanity through space and time is in his view "but the empirical and external manifestation of the immanent eternal victory, the full and absolute victory of mind over nature."[3]

The Hegelian tradition undergoes a significant modification in the hands of Bradley and Bosanquet. They agree that the temporal scheme of change falls as an essential factor within the supreme synthesis of the non-temporal Absolute. It is essential because changing appearances are the "stuff" of which reality is made. But although changing appearances are, in a sense, the stuff of reality, they are obviously self-contradictory appearances. They owe their existence to the finitude of the human mind, to the discriminating activity of human thought. In the supra-rational experience of the Absolute, changes are

---

[1] Josiah Royce, *The World and the Individual,* 2nd Series (London: The Macmillan & Co., 1929), p. 141.

[2] Giovanni Gentile, *The Theory of Mind as Pure Act* (London: Macmillan & Co., 1922), p. 209.

[3] Ibid., p. 250.

transformed beyond recognition. In the timeless perfection of the real, time is a radically transmuted process. Past, present and future exist only for the finite mind. In the all-comprehensive experience of the Absolute they blend together into an Eternal Now.

But with the distinctions of past and future gone, strictly speaking, even the concept of the present or the "eternal now" loses its meaning. From the standpoint of the absolute, even the distinction of time and eternity is reduced to a nullity.

Doctrine of Change as Ultimately Real

According to idealism, then, change is unreal in some sense or other. Time is a prisoner in the house of the spirit. Reality in its essential structure is timeless perfection. But at the opposite end of the philosophical spectrum is the doctrine of change as ultimate reality. In modern Western thought Henri Bergson leads the way to the reaffirmation of the Heraclitean doctrine of universal flux. Bergson takes his stand upon the ultimate reality of change, change which is conceived as total and perpetual, pure and undiluted. Change is, in his view, emphatically not a mere element in the superior reality of permanence; it is rather permanence which is an abstraction from the continuous flow of change. The indisputable fact of change can by no means be explained as a stream of static phases or immobile positions of a persistent entity. Immobilities without number placed in endless juxtaposition can by no trick produce the appearance of mobility. But it is quite possible to carve out of the continuous mobility of the real an endless number of immobile views or static snapshots.

This is abundantly illustrated by the operation of the cinematograph. In order to transcribe the movement of a thing, say, a marching regiment of soldiers, the cinematograph first obtains a sufficiently large number of snapshots of the moving regiment of soldiers in their different positions. These static snapshots placed in juxtaposition in a definite order have then to be put into the movement of a machine in order to produce the appearance of a moving picture. This clearly shows that even an artificial reproduction of motion requires the introduction of real motion somewhere. Static or immobile elements, however numerous, are essentially incapable of generating mobility; nay, they are incapable of producing even the illusion of mobility without the aid of some real motion. Thus, it follows, that permanence can neither be the source of change, nor an essential factor in the nature of change. It is just a characteristic of an abstract view of change. It is a derivative of change traceable to the cinematographic mechanism of thought. While instability is the essence of concrete actuality, stability belongs to the region of abstract possibility.

But if motion, change, time, or development, embodies the final truth of things, how is it that thought which is concerned with knowledge and truth should pervert it into a mere moving image of the Eternal? How can the very organ of knowledge be a deliberate attempt to obscure knowledge into a tissue of errors? Bergson answers this question with an emphatic repudiation of the view that thought is an organ of knowledge. In his opinion the faculty by virtue of which one can feel the pulse of reality in its creative flow is not thought, but intuition. While thought moves 'round and round' an object in a mist of uncertainty, intuition alone can take one straight to the heart of things. Thought is, in Bergson's view, a mere pragmatic function, a tool of practical life fashioned in the course of evolution. The categories of thought, therefore, answer to necessities of practical life. Permanence or stability is the essence of all such categories. Action is not possible where everything is in constant flux. In order to render action possible, we require points of rest in the flux of events; we require to proceed from rest to rest so that we may control and regulate our movements. That is why in surveying the movement of a thing, thought is chiefly concerned with its possible or imaginary stopping places, or with static snapshots thereof.

Then again, that which is most important in practical life is the fulfillment of some desire or the attainment of some definite end. The means which are adopted are entirely subordinate to the goal or end. The end is in essence the negation of movement; it brings movement to restful termination. It is, therefore, natural that in active life our attention should be fixed upon the immobile ends of our movement. Whereas, the immobility of the starting point supplies the basis for a possible course of action, the immobility of the goal or design imparts to that course of action its order and definite direction. Herein lies the source of inspiration for intellectualist philosophy. Intellectualism ignores the pragmatic character of thought and glorifies it as the essential structure of reality. It conceives of the unchanging eternal as the alpha and omega, the first cause and the final reason of the flux of empirical existence.

Bergson maintains that a complete reversal of the intellectual bent of the mind in favor of intuitive penetration into the heart of reality would produce a radical transformation of our outlook. We then realize that it is not permanence but change which is the real essence of all things. Turning our gaze inwards within ourselves we can immediately perceive that our psychical existence means continuous change. "To exist is to change, to change is to mature, to mature is to go on creating one's self endlessly."[4] Thus, the world of life and mind is undoubtedly a process of change. It is the process of continuous making and remaking.

The material world also is no exception to this fundamental law of existence. Matter is, however, in Bergson's opinion, continually unmaking itself. It is moving and changing in the direction opposite to that of life. It is the process of running down while life is the process of rising up. There is ample corroboration of this view from

---

[4] Henri Bergson, *Creative Evolution*, p. 8.

the side of science today. Modern physics has resolved matter entirely into energy, into the vibratory motion of charges of electricity. And the second law of thermo-dynamics has brought to light the gradual degradation of the energy of the material world. Bergson holds that change which is the essence of reality is pure, perpetual and total. Change is perpetual in the sense that there is a radical recasting of the entire reality going on at every moment. It is total in the sense that it extends to the whole of existence, to everything that is real, to matter, life, mind, and other things. Change is pure in the sense that it does not imply any persistent entity or unchanging thing that changes. The so-called 'thing' is in point of truth a period of change taken in a block. The alleged principle of permanence-in-change is, in Bergson's judg-ment, only a practical, useful construction of the intellect, But this pure change is not to be construed as abstract, colorless change, or as the featureless generality of be-coming. Bergson takes care to guard against this possible misconstruction. Change or becoming, which is the soul of reality, is conceived by him as infinitely variegated becoming. It is the interpenetration of an infinite wealth of content ever marching into the future. "An infinite multiplicity of becoming, variously colored, so to speak, passes before our eyes."[5]

Bergson distinguishes between qualitative movements, evolutionary movements, and extensive movements. And he shows how they differ profoundly from one and an-other. That which goes from yellow to green is not like that which goes from green to blue; they are different qualitative movements. That which goes from flower to fruit is not like that which goes from larva to nymph and from nymph to perfect insect; they are different evolu-tionary movements. The action of eating or drinking is not like the action of fighting; they are different extensive movements. In Bergson's considered opinion, the funda-mental principle of change, the vital impetus, is not a

[5] Ibid., p. 321.

blank, featureless entity, but something like an explosive energy which bears within itself an unstable balance of divergent tendencies.

The outstanding merit of Bergson is that he is a forceful representative of the spirit of the modern age. Dynamism is indeed the characteristic tendency of present times. The notions of activity and change, becoming and process, receive today much emphasis and significance. The concept of evolution is erected into an ultimate metaphysical category, and we hear today not only of a philosophy of evolution, but of evolutional philosophy. The truth of absolute being lies, in the judgment of many modern thinkers, in absolute becoming, and we have on this point a meeting of radical extremes in contemporary philosophy. Vitalists, pragmatists, new idealists, and new realists, have all joined their voices to swell one mighty current of evolutionary outlook. They are votaries of change, high priests of evolution.

Some of the causes which have served to bring about this energetic reaction from the classical tradition in philosophy may be briefly stated here.

In the first place, there is a maximum intensification in modern life of the struggle for existence. There is a rapid disappearance of the scope for armchair reflection, and cloistered contemplation. A spirit of restless activity and incessant drive is to be noticed everywhere.

Secondly, in a new awakening to the higher values of life, there is an overemphasis on the moral point of view, and an acceptance of moral values as final and supreme. The moral point of view translates perfection into unending perfectibility, and therefore is inclined to look upon ultimate reality as an unceasing creative effort and not as an eternal calm. Dr. Bosanquet rightly remarks in this connection: "the very extremes of philosophy, insofar as it assumes the character of a philosophy of change, concentrate themselves round the moral point of view. The moral point of view is that in which man takes his realization in an endless process, and so perpetually feels the impulse to transcend his existing reality."[6]

Finally, the present age is a period of critical transition through which humanity is passing. It is a preparation for the next saltus in evolution. The philosophy of change is the first reaction of the reflective mind to the consciously felt urge of evolution. The stubborn fact of change is felt to be a positive refutation of the postulate of permanence at the heart of reality.

William James ridicules the absolutist's conception of reality as a "Block Universe", and points out that the world process is necessarily reduced in absolutist philosophy to a mere "dull rattling off of a chain forged innumerable years ago." He formulates his view of the world as a concatenated series of changes, and holds that it is a living, moving, and growing part of the universe that we inhabit.

Croce, the neoidealist, emphasizes the endless perfectibility of man and speaks of the "endless dialectic of the spirit." He conceives of reality as infinite possibility flowing into an infinite actuality as a continual surpassing of itself. He equates reality with history.

Samuel Alexander, the neorealist, looks upon the world as an all-encompassing system of motion, a scheme of perpetual change and restless striving. Even the deity of religion is, in his opinion, only a future possibility with which the universe is in travail and towards which it is constantly straining forward.

Alfred North Whitehead emphasizes the actual world as a continuous passage of events, as activity ever merging into the future, as the creative advance of nature. He interprets this creative advance, not as a succession of instantaneous events, not as perpetual recreation at each instant, but as a temporal, indivisible complex of activity with internal relations between its various factors. He expresses great delight at the emancipation of modern physics from the Newtonian conception of nature. All

[6] Bernard Bosanquet, *The Meeting of Extremes in Contemporary Philosophy* (Macmillan and Co. Ltd., 1924), p. 214.

interrelations of matters of fact must, in his view, involve transition in their essence.[7] He speaks, no doubt, of eternal objects, but these eternal objects are supposed by him to belong to the realm of possibility. They can be said to be real only insofar as they are capable of being "ingressed" into the passage of events or actual entities.

Criticism of the Doctrine of Change

The doctrine of the exclusive reality of change cannot, however, bear the light of critical examination. Change is, without doubt, a fact *within* the universe, but that gives no warrant for concluding that it is a fact *of* the universe, or that it is the final truth about the totality of all being. The concept of change is a limited concept inasmuch as it is limited in its application to phenomena of the world. It does not apply to the world as the unity of all phenomena. The whole of the universe can hardly be conceived in terms of expansion or diminution; nor can it ever depart from its fundamental nature and structure. "The whole of what exists cannot move away from its fundamental characters—say its categories—and values".[8]

Change is without doubt an essential characteristic in the universe, but it does not follow that change is the whole truth about the universe. The very affirmation that change alone is real is intended to be an eternal truth. Thus, the apostles of change are confuted out of their own mouth. To deny permanence as an aspect of reality is to affirm one's belief in a permanent truth about reality. Eternalism and temporalism are thus complementary half truths. They represent two inseparable aspects of the same reality.

Bergson is right in pointing out that much of our thinking is pragmatic in function and outlook. But he ignores the truth that thought is a self-transcending activity of

---

[7] Alfred North Whitehead, *Modes of Thought* (Cambridge: Cambridge University Press, 1938), p. 200.

[8] Bernard Bosanquet, op. cit., p. 193.

man. It has a purely theoretical as well as a practical side. It is quite capable of rising above the limitations of practical life and commanding a detached view of the fundamental structure of reality. The unchangeableness of Reality in respect of its fundamental structure is disclosed, not by the pragmatic understanding, but by the pure reason.

This disclosure of the pure reason is further reinforced by the spiritual intuitions of mankind. Mystic seers the world over are in full agreement with speculative thinkers in affirming the reality of the eternal as an essential aspect of the Real.

It is true that particular things and objects of the world are always changing. But it is no less true, that certain patterns, certain structural forms, always abide and repeat themselves in the midst of all changes. Then again, there are some basic laws of nature which unchangingly regulate all the changes of nature. Truths which are verified as true about the temporality of the world are non-temporal. The supreme values of life, such as truth, beauty, goodness, freedom, unity, etc. are like the beacon light of Eternity on life's voyage on the sea of change. As objects of devoted appreciation, they form the shining goal of the pyramid of knowledge. A refusal to admit the objective and supreme reality of these values would amount to a wholesale condemnation of the most central experiences of mankind, such as science, art, morality and religion.

Absolute Dualism of Change and Permanence

Some philosophers, such as Prof. C. E. M. Joad frankly admit the reality of both change and permanence. They represent them as two entirely separate and discontinuous spheres of reality. In their view, there is a yawning chasm between the dynamic flux of change and the static realm of eternal perfection. Neither can actual entities be said to participate in eternal Forms, nor can eternal Forms be

said to "ingress" into actual occasions and thus to contribute actively to their shaping and molding. The relation between the world of change and the world of permanence is conceived by Joad as one of "nonsignificant
resemblance." By this he means that it is a matter of
arbitrary contingent fact that some physical objects appear
to imitate the eternal ideal Form. No rational explanation can be afforded of this fact of imitation in terms
of an organic relation or causal connection between the
two spheres of reality. Joad considers it impossible "that
the unchanging can enter into and give shape to the changing, without either itself partaking of the nature of change,
or causing the changing to take on some of the character
of the changeless." All that one can say is that the actual
world includes certain constituents which exhibit certain
qualities. It is a matter of brute contingency that these
qualities appear as a selection from an infinite realm of
possibility.

The above doctrine of absolute bifurcation of reality
into the changing and the unchanging violently clashes
with our fundamental conviction about the unity of all
existence. It is due to our perception of the basic unity
of all existence that no sooner do we posit the Many than
we proceed to bring together the elements of the Many
by some sort of interaction or organic connection. With
regard to particulars and universals, Plato's doctrine of
"participation," and Whitehead's theory of "ingression"
are examples to the point. Had the changing and the unchanging been entirely separate and discontinuous in
being, it would have been impossible for the changing
mind to have any cognitive contact with the changeless
world of universal values. Knowledge presupposes the
identity of being or confluence of existence. Moreover,
it would have been impossible for a man to give concrete
shape and embodiment in the changing world to his
vision of the idea, if the changing material were not adapt-
able to the idea, or if the ideal had no effective power
of control over the actual. In his eagerness to do justice

to both the terms of the antithesis, Joad puts them on two sides of an unbridgeable discontinuity.

Change and Permanence as Two Dimensions of Being

It, therefore, seems to us that the view which looks upon change and permanence as separate and discontinuous spheres of existence, and the view which reduces one of them to a mere illusory shadow of the other, are equally unsatisfactory extremes of thought. The changing and the unchanging, the dynamic and the static (*kṣara* and *akṣara*) are, in our judgment, two poises of being, two equally real modes of manifestation, of the same Supreme Being.

Whitehead is right when he says that eternal objects are elements of possibility which are capable of being actualized. But these elements of possibility are not like floating entities; they are possibilities inherent in the structure of Being. In the course of time, selections from these infinite possibilities are made for actualization in the changing world. The changing world cannot be condemned as unreal even from the ultimate standpoint. It is, as we have seen, a genuine manifestation of the self-expansive, creative joy of Being.

The ultimate truth is neither change nor permanence, neither time nor eternity. The ultimate truth lies in the multidimensional fullness of Being. When a person one-sidedly starts with the abstract concept of eternity, he feels intellectually constrained to demonstrate time as unreal. When, on the contrary, he one-sidedly starts with the abstract concept of time, he feels an inner compulsion to repudiate eternity as an illusion. It is when we are guided from the very beginning with an integral view of Being in its multidimensional fullness that we can hope to understand philosophically the total truth as the identity of change and permanence, of the temporal and the eternal.

Chapter 9

THE MEANING OF EVOLUTION

Evolution does not mean mere change. The concept of evolution is far greater than that of mere change or passage of events. It signifies change of a specified character, change for the higher and the better. It means development, creative advance, continual enrichment of being, progressive manifestation of ever higher and more desirable qualities.

The theory of evolution represents the movement of time as an upward curve of development which gradually unfolds unsuspected treasures and brings into existence ever higher values. In the doctrine of evolution, time is thus credited with a vast, creative importance. It is indeed regarded as the very principle of creativity.

Evolution does not merely consist of progress within the limits of a particular species. It implies the emergence of higher and higher species, endowed with new emergent qualities.

Besides gradual self-development, evolution implies perpetual self-overcoming and self-transcending. It is the increasing self-fulfillment of the cosmic creative urge in and through different types of self and different kinds of species.

That is why it has been possible for a lower species of animal to evolve into a higher species of animal. It has been possible for the animal to evolve into the human form. And it is also perhaps quite possible for man to evolve one day into the superman or the divine man.

It is possible that there are other planes of cosmic existence, supraphysical or preternatural planes. But these are all probably typal in character, and not, strictly speaking, evolutionary. Supraphysical planes of existence allow for progress of some sort, for growing self-fulfillment within the limits of fixed types. But there is no scope in them for self-exceeding and development into radically different types. In terrestrial evolution, however, there is not only progress of individuals within the limits set by their class essence, there is also the bursting of the universal life force beyond the limits defined by class patterns. There are various modes of self-fulfillment through self-transcendence. That is why we witness here boundless varieties of species, which can all be arranged in a hierarchical order, and in which the higher species is believed to evolve out of the lower species.

Sri Aurobindo has made a significant contribution to the concept of evolution, and has thrown a flood of light upon the nature and significance of terrestrial evolution. He holds that there are different orders of self-fulfillment of the Supreme Being. There are, for instance, supernal worlds of infinity—worlds of infinite existence, infinite consciousness, and infinite delight—in everyone of which one of the infinite components of ultimate reality functions as the basic and dominant principle. There are also worlds or planes in which the Supermind functions as the basic and dominant principle. Again, there are purely mental planes in which the mind functions as the basic and dominant principle. All these worlds or planes are typal in nature. They are fields of manifestation of fixed types, and whatever takes place in them is in the nature of increasing self-expression within the limits of these types. Mystics the world over bear affirmative witness to such supraterrestrial spheres of existence, or planes of consciousness. Vedic seers speak of seven worlds,—the worlds of matter (Bhuḥ), life (Bhuvaḥ), mind (Svaḥ), Supermind (Mahā), pure delight (Jana), pure consciousness-force (Tapas), and pure being (Satya). The material world is that in which matter functions as the basic and dominant principle. The material world is essentially evolutionary in character, while the other worlds are typal in nature.

In the scheme of evolution characteristic of the material world the point of departure is matter, and the purpose of evolution is to bring forth into full revelation the riches of the Supreme under the conditions provided by matter. But is it bare matter empty of all other principles which is to serve as the point of departure and the nurse of all becoming? That would have led to the stultification of reason and would have rendered inexplicable the emergence of life, mind, etc. one after another, in ordered succession. That would have left the cosmic drift without any significant driving force which might give it a definite direction. We have no objection to admit with Tyndall that "matter contains the promise and potency of the whole of terrestrial life." Only, we must add that this matter is not what we, in our profound ignorance, take it to be; it is the most primordial form of manifestation of Being. It is the grossest form of manifestation of the element of infinite being, or existentiality (Sat) in ultimate reality which is in the nature of being-conscious-ness-delight (*Saccidānanda*).

It should be further noted that the seven or eight principles of which the web of existence is woven are identical in being, even though they may be diverse in outward action. So in the stuff of matter which constitutes the starting-point of terrestrial evolution there must be involved from the very beginning all the other component principles of ultimate reality. Having descended through gradual self-alienation into the inconscience of matter, the Spirit gets involved therein with all the other elements of its nature. It is this *involution* of all in one which constitutes the necessity of *evolution* and imparts a specific direction to the cosmic drift. It is because life energy is already involved in matter in a form suited to it—in the subvital form, as Sri Aurobindo puts it—that life appears in its distinctive form at a subsequent stage of evolution. Similarly, it is because mind is already involved in matter and life that the force of evolution can, in fullness of time, bring it forth into explicit manifestation. The evolutionary self-expression of the Spirit has thus, for its necessary presupposition, the involutionary self-conceal-ment of the Spirit in nature.

The above theory of evolution aims to reconcile the timeless perfection of Being with the temporal process of the world. It also reconciles the notions of evolution as a teleological process and as an absolutely free act of crea-tion.

Evolution has been conceived by some as an asymptotic approximation to an infinite ideal. This is evidently in-spired by an exclusive stress upon the moral point of view, which drives a wedge of separation between the actual and the ideal. This gives out the notion of a *progressus ad infinitum,* in which the gates of the future are ever open. But a slight reflection will show that a *progressus ad in-finitum* is a contradiction in terms. When the goal is ever-receding and always illusive, like the horizon, there is no meaning in an increasing approximation thereto. The theory of evolution as an endless approximation to an unattainable goal is opposed by those who believe in a definite consummation of the march of evolution. They put forward what may be called the theory of *progressus ad finitum,* which implies faith in a "far-off divine event to which the whole of creation moves." Faith in such a finality of achievement would mean a shutting of the gates of the future. Dr. McTaggart speaks of the futurity of the whole,[1] and believes in the resolution of the time series sustained by ignorance in the timeless perception of truth to be attained at a certain future date. Mr. Joad holds that the final goal of evolution is unfettered con-templation of the world of values by humanity as a whole and that this goal is not impossible of achievement.[2] But

---

[1] John McTaggart, *The Nature of Existence,* Vol. II (Cambridge: The University Press, 1927), Ch. LXI.

[2] C.E.M. Joad, *Matter, Life and Value,* p. 374.

to suggest that the attainment of a definite goal is the last word about the process of evolution is to ignore the infinite character and inexhaustible richness of Being. Finality of achievement is incompatible with the infinity of the Real.

Croce therefore maintains that the true conception of progress must steer clear of the opposite extremes of an aim completely attained, and an aim essentially unattainable. It must avoid the one-sidedness of *progressus ad finitum* on the one hand, and that of *progressus ad infinitum* on the other. Progress rightly conceived is, according to Croce, "a perpetual solution and a perpetually renascent problem demanding a new solution."[3] At every instant, there is an attainment of the true and the good, and there is the raising of a doubt at every fresh instant, without however losing what has been attained.

Now, with regard to a definite goal, if it be said to be automatically realized at every moment of advance, then either it is not, as Joad points out, a goal at all truly so-called, but merely a part of the process, or, there is no real advance. When there is a fixed goal, it cannot perpetually obtain realization and yet await realization. It seems to us that the course of terrestrial evolution is throughout controlled by the idea of a definite goal—the goal of a certain mode of manifestation of Being in terrestrial conditions. From the standpoint of this goal, the evolution of man into superman, or the race of gnostic beings would be a great advance. But, the attainment of this goal would not mean cessation of further progression in time. In the first place, it would mean replacement of progression in the Ignorance by progression in the Knowledge. While progression in the Ignorance is a zigzag course, a slow and protracted evolution through ups and downs, an uphill journey through serious errors and setbacks, progression in the Knowledge would be a rapid transformation, a triumphant march from truth to truth,

---

[3] C.E.M. Joad, *Introduction to Modern Philosophy* (Oxford: The Clarendon Press, 1925), p. 43.

and from glory to glory. The end of evolution in the Ignorance would indeed herald the dawn of a new era of infinitely variable self-expression in truth and love and beauty. In the second place, the complete fruition of the present cycle of evolution would perhaps be followed by other cycles of evolution, other modes of evolutionary self-fulfillment.

Thus we see that evolution can very well be conceived as an increasing manifestation of the infinite richness of Being. The infinite richness of Being presents itself to the temporal point of view as an endless variety of definite goals or purposes. Each of these purposes presides over a particular cycle of evolution. Just as there is no dead finality about the process of evolution, so also on the other hand, evolution is no indefinitely prolonged endless drift or fruitless pursuit of an ever-receding ideal. It is quite possible, as we have just now indicated, to reconcile the notion of fixed and definite goals with that of infinite progression in time.

Sri Aurobindo's theory of evolution as the Supermind's progressive self-manifestation in infinitely diverse conditions does also embody a reconciliation of the reality of the world process with the eternal perfection of the Spirit. It does not reduce the flux of sensible existence, either to an illusion or to "a tale told by an idiot full of sound and fury signifying nothing". Nor, does it reduce it to a degradation or diminution of the essence of Being, or to the repetition of paradise lost and paradise regained. True, the Supreme descends down the slope of self-alienation in order to take a plunge into the inconscience of matter. But this adventurous plunge into the inconscience is prompted by the purpose of self-manifestation in terms of matter. True, the evolutionary descent is followed by evolutionary ascent, but that does not amount to a vicious circle. Because the reascent of evolution does not aim at merely getting the Spirit back to its original timeless perfection of unitary experience. Evolution aims at progressive unveiling of the Spirit in ever unique sets of conditions. The purpose of cosmic evolution is a kind of purposeless purpose. It is the purpose of creative joy, of Being's joyful self-expression. It is not procuring something from without, but objectifying something from within. It is actualizing the riches of inwardness. It is the spontaneous outflow of inward fullness. After a day's hard labor and weariness, when a person takes a hearty meal and relaxes on the sofa, he begins to feel again very full inside. What does he want to do then? Out of a sense of inward fullness, he may feel like singing or dancing, or writing poetry or playing a game. Such activities are neither meaningless nor utilitarian. They are a joyful outpouring of the inner self. Similarly, evolution is a spontaneous unfoldment of the creative urge of Being.

Evolution as Emergence of Novelties

It will not be out of place to institute here a brief comparison between Sri Aurobindo's theory of terrestrial evolution as progressive self-manifestation of the Supreme in material conditions and Prof. S. Alexander's theory of emergent evolution.

Prof. Alexander looks upon matter, not as the basic stuff of existence, but as the first emergent quality which comes to qualify specific configurations of spatiotemporal elements or events. But while, according to Alexander, that which is prior to matter, that which functions as "the matrix of all existence and the nurse of all becoming," is hyphenated space-time conceived as a comprehensive system of motion, Sri Aurobindo identifies this ultimate principle as unfathomable Being, of which space-time is the medium of self-expression.

Being is not space-time but the ground of all existence in space-time. Being is not mind, or reason, or thought, but the creative source of them. Being is not love or joy or beauty, but the sustaining ground of them. As the root and basis of all existence, knowledge and joy, Being may, from our human standpoint, be defined as infinite existence-knowledge-bliss *(Saccidānanda)*.

Prof. Einstein is perfectly right when he says that space-time is not itself the basic stuff but rather a form of some more ultimate stuff or substance, the precise nature of which is more than science can determine. Sri Aurobindo maintains that space and time are cosmic forms of the Infinite's self-extension and self-revelation. They are the media in which the Supreme Being pours out its inexhaustible riches and spreads out its infinite being. Infinite space and infinite time are in essence *a priori* forms, whether forms of existence or forms of perception. So, no amount of hyphenating will convert them into the ultimate stuff or creative principle of the world.

Alexander regards matter, life, mind, etc. as a series of emergent qualities which appear on the scene of empirical reality on the attainment of an increasingly greater degree of complexity of structure and function on the part of point-instants or events. But, as to the source of these unique emergent qualities, he leaves us completely in the dark. The fact of emergence he is inclined to treat as a miracle, and he invites us to accept it as the final inexplicability. But that is hard for reason to swallow. Belief in miracles, in whatever form, has no respectable place in philosophical thinking.

Dr. Pringle-Pattison has tried to explain the emergence of qualitative differences by tracing them to the hitherto unmanifest riches of the Absolute. He holds that the series of emergent qualities are the "progressive revelation"[4] on the empirical plane of the inexhaustible riches of the eternal.

The view of Pringle-Pattison is surely an improvement on Alexander's conception of the matter, but there is a serious defect lurking even in this position. According to Pringle-Pattison, as also according to Alexander, the emergent qualities emanate from without or from above, and do not gradually evolve from within. They are, as it

---

[4] A Seth Pringle-Pattison, *The Idea of God*, (New York: Oxford University Press, 1920), p. 154.

were, thrust into the evolutionary series at certain critical stages. They are not conceived to have any organic connection with their substructure. Life, for instance, supervenes from above having no organic relationship to its material substructure. Likewise, mind is a supervenient perfection having no strictly organic connection with its vital or nervous substructure.

The facts of experience flatly contradict any such lack of organic continuity. It is not true that a configuration of purely material processes comes to be qualified mysteriously by an extraneous quality of vitality at a higher stage of evolution. The life energy is in point of truth an organically related aspect of physical forces, having been secretly operative in matter from the very beginning. It does not supervene from above. Having been always latent in matter, it becomes overtly operative in living beings in the course of evolution. Similarly, it is not true that a specific configuration of purely vital processes comes to be qualified by mentality thrust into it, as it were, from without or from above. Mentality was already present in the lower forms of organism in a submental or subconscious form. In the fullness of time, it is brought into explicit self-realization by the forward march of evolution.

The fresh novelties which appear in the course of evolution are neither miracles nor supervenient surprises. They are not devoid of organic connection with their substructure. They are in the nature of the outflowering of such factors as were implicitly operative in the lower levels from the very beginning. It was possible for them to emerge in the course of evolution only because they were already involved in matter as closely interwoven aspects of one and the same reality.

Similarly, intelligence is implicitly present in the animal consciousness. In the course of evolution, when empirical conditions become suitable, when the appropriate nervous system is perfected, intelligence becomes overtly operative, resulting in the emergence of man as a distinct species.

The Nisus of Evolution

It is now clear that it is because life, mind, spirit, etc. had already been involved in the inconscience of matter that the march of evolution could bring them forth in successive order into explicit self-fulfillment. But though the fact of involution gives a certain necessity and a definite orientation to the course of evolution, it is not sufficient to account for the creative impulse of evolution. Let us therefore turn now our attention to a consideration of the creative impulse or nisus of evolution. Let us try to have an idea of that which constitutes the driving power behind the evolutionary process.

Various attempts have been made in philosophy to account for the process of evolution—its nisus and its determinate order—without resorting to any principle of cosmic intelligence or conscious teleology. Professor Alexander says that the drive of evolution is to be traced to a creative nisus, an initial urge, with which space-time is originally endowed. But whence is this creative nisus in space-time? The presence of the creative impulse in space-time seems to point to the reality of some fundamental cosmic energy, of which space-time is in ultimate analysis the medium of self-expression. And that cosmic energy cannot be blind and mechanical. The world of space-time as an evolutionary scheme shows evidence of order and direction. So, the cosmic energy must be endowed with some kind of ordering intelligence. The emergence of novel forms in the course of evolution indicates the immanence of some formative power in the basic creative energy. Professor Radhakrishnan is perfectly right when he observes: "Unless we assume the nisus to be a spiritual power ever drawing on its resources and ever expressing new forms, Alexander's whole account becomes unsatisfactory."[5]

---

[5] S. Radhakrishnan, *An Idealistic View of Life* (London: George Allen & Unwin Ltd., 1932), p. 323.

Bergson has not much difficulty with the problem of nisus insofar as his ultimate principle is itself a creative nisus, an infinite, vital surge, an *élan vital*. But Bergson's *élan vital* is too determinate a principle to function as the philosophical ultimate. Having defined the fundamental creative energy as the life force, Bergson finds himself under the necessity of explaining matter on the one hand, and the mind and spirit on the other, in terms of life-force. But life can no more explain matter than matter can explain life. Likewise, mind or reason can no more explain the existence of matter and life than matter or life can explain mind or reason. In order to account for the emergence of matter, life, mind, spirit, as distinctive values, the ultimate creative energy must not be identified with any one of them.

Chapter 10

THE GOAL OF EVOLUTION

It has been noted before that we can think of change without any definite direction or goal. But we cannot think of evolution apart from some goal, finite or infinite. Evolution is definitely a goal-oriented process. It is the emergence of ever-new higher qualities, forms and values.

Now the term 'higher' has no meaning unless we accept some intrinsic and absolute values as the most desirable end of all process and change. For instance, we consider life as higher than matter, because a living organism shows certain characteristics of self-existence which is accepted as the ideal and most perfect mode of being. It has the powers of self-regulation, self-healing, immanent self-development from within, self-reproduction, etc. Similarly, we consider mind as higher than life, because it shows further characteristics of self-existence. It has greater self-movement, flexibility of response, self-adjustment to changing circumstances, etc. Rational consciousness is considered a still higher quality, because it can change outward circumstances to suit the requirements of inner life. It can initiate entirely new changes calculated to secure optimum happiness, to produce increasing knowledge, power, harmony and cooperation, and to open wider vistas of truth, beauty, love and freedom.

Now, the question is, How does the goal operate in the process of evolution? Much of man's deliberate action is characterized by conscious and rational planning. But it would be sheer anthropomorphism to attribute the human kind of rational planning to Nature. Gone are the days when a carpenter theory of creation or a watchmaker theory of evolution could be accepted, postulating an omnipotent Mind up there somewhere beyond Nature. Attempts to understand the creativity of Nature after the fashion of man's conscious teleology are bound to appear anachronistic today.

Moreover, it appears upon deeper reflection that even the plans and designs of man's rational mind are not the ultimate moving force in his life. They seem rather to be reflections at the level of the rational mind of much deeper unconscious motivations. Unfathomed forces working from the depths of his inner psyche seem to be the prime mover of his life. There are clear indications that man's conscious teleology is only an imperfect instrumentation of some enormously vast unconscious or superconscious intelligence immanently operative at the very center of life and nature.

In consideration of the unknown forces immanently regulating the process of evolution, various theories of unconscious and superconscious teleology have been propounded. It might be rewarding to consider here briefly some of these views.

Theory of Unconscious Teleology

We come across a theory of unconscious teleology in the *Sāṅkhya* system of Indian philosophy. According to the *Sāṅkhya*, Nature is essentially and completely unconscious (*jaḍa*). Yet there are significant happenings in Nature. There are valuable results emerging in implicit obedience to natural laws. Now, the Sānkhya believes that behind all the workings of nature is the constant presence of a detached but ever-awake onlooker, a self-luminous spirit (*puruṣa*), for whose sake nature works and to whose contact her evolution owes its initial start. This gives a different complexion to the Sānkhya doctrine of unconscious teleology, and sharply distinguishes it from the theories of unconscious teleology which we find in western philosophy. According to the Sānkhya, even though the primal stuff and the driving power of evolution is intrinsically unconscious, the principle that silently presides over the course of evolution, that which affords inspiration and also lends significance to the evolutionary urge, is an eternally perfect, self-subsistent principle of consciousness.

Mr. Hoernle's attitude to the problem of teleology has been crystalized into the formula "not mechanism or vitalism, but mechanism and teleology."[1] He admits that every new order of existence, such as life or mind, is without doubt the outcome of a mechanistic scheme of things and the result of unconscious forces. There is no need to posit any intelligent principle of consciousness to preside over the mechanically determined course of events. But we may speak of teleology in the sense that after a new order of existence appears on the scene, we find it supremely valuable and desirable. It is this valuable and desirable character of the new product of evolution which justifies our language of teleology. Since the values are not only intrinsically good but also necessary facts by reason of being rigorously determined, the total scheme of the universe cannot be said to be quite indifferent to those which it produces and sustains.

Now, a little reflection will show that the above view involves an attempt to hide the real difficulty about the matter and to cover it under a mist of misleading phrases. The position of Hoernle is, to put it plainly, that there is only mechanism, and that life, mind, etc. result from the conjunction of mechanical forces, albeit these mechanically produced things may also be immensely valuable in our human eyes. And it is precisely here that the sting of the problem lies. How can an ascending series of supreme values, such as life, mind, and personality, be brought into being by a set of blind forces which are blind without qualification? To speak of an unconscious teleology in this sense, is simply to state the fact without any attempt at explanation.

---

[1] Hoernle, *Studies in Contemporary Metaphysics*, Chaps. VI and VII.

Theory of Superconscious Teleology

Dr. Bosanquet speaks of superconscious as well as unconscious forms of teleology, in addition to the conscious teleology of human activity.[2] Bosanquet holds that explicitly conscious teleology which we notice at the human level is, far from being the only type and vehicle of teleology, only an intermediate form of expression of a deeper teleology, which is operative in the cosmic process. The beautiful flower that we admire is neither a chance product thrown off by the wanton play of blind forces, nor a miracle superinduced on the course of things by an arbitrary will of God. It is rather the immanent development of its own environment in which His plan was deeply imbedded. This is unconscious teleology characteristic of the infrahuman levels of nature.

Similarly, there is superconscious teleology which is exemplified in such superindividual structures as a civilization or the political organization of a state. Take any civilization of the present day you like, and it will be immediately evident that it was never explicitly present in all its present proportions and significance to the consciousness of any single individual or group of individuals. But still there can be no disputing the fact that it is not an accidental formation, but the concrete realization of a deeper purpose immanent in the scheme of reality. It is the fulfillment of a profounder plan which has worked through the coordination of the conscious activities of generations of people. The apparent motives of our human actions provide the instrumentation through which the deeper plan of history operates.

Even in the case of finite conscious teleology it is the deeper plan which is of capital importance. The aim which is constantly held before our minds undergoes continuous modification and reshaping under the pressure of the secret nature of things as we press forward with our

work of self-realization. The *de facto* end is, as Dr. Bosanquet is never tired of reiterating, never the thing of
primary or decisive importance. It is always determined
by the nature of a system, part of which has already been
actualized, and the residual part of which awaits realization for the completion of the whole. So, Bosanquet concludes that "teleology is only a sub-form of harmony".
There are teleological movements in nature inasmuch as
there is immanent in every finite part a spirit of harmony,
or a principle of totality which impels it to a self-transcending, and consequently to a fuller self-realizing. The
deeper plan in the nature of things is the result of the
all-pervasive immanence of the Absolute in the universe.

Now, this deeper plan cannot, we submit, be in any
way inferior to our finite consciousness. It must in truth
be infinitely superior to human intelligence. It must be
a kind of super-conscious intelligence. To use a significant expression of Sri Aurobindo, it is "the superconscient
creative energy" of Being.

Modus Operandi of Superconscious Teleology

It is then the superconscient energy of Being which
constitutes the real nisus of the onward march of evolution. But the dynamism of Being operates not wantonly
and arbitrarily, but through a machinery of laws and
forces. In shaping the course of evolution, the creative
energy functions through two closely cooperating forces.

First, there is an *upward-tending force from below* bringing forth into articulate expression an ascending series of
ever-new qualities, powers and values. This upward drive
results from the involution of the higher into the lower,
the involution of the Spirit in mind, of mind in life, and
of life in matter. Secondly, there is an *upward-drawing
force from above* which results from the constant pressure
exerted by the higher orders of existence upon the lower.
This pressure and the consequent upward-drawing attrac-
tion not only help and accelerate the upward-tending
force from below but also very largely determine the spe-

cial ways in which it is eventually realized.

We have already seen that the material world of our experience is, as Sri Aurobindo points out, only one among a large variety of distinct modes of self-fulfillment of the Supreme Being. Whereas, in the material world, matter is the dominant principle and the starting point of the evolutionary process, with other principles involved in it and gradually evolving from it, there are most probably other orders of Being's self-fulfillment. In one of them life may function as the dominant principle. In another still it is perhaps the Supermind which functions as the principal determinant. This separate dominance of different principles of being in different planes of existence is not only a philosophic possibility, but a verifiable reality to which many mystics bear affirmative witness. The cooperation of the upward-tending force from below and the upward-drawing force from above in determining the course of evolution is specially in evidence in the history of human self-development. Man has a more or less vivid awareness of an irrepressible urge from within and also of uplifting and ennobling forces from above. The higher a man ascends on the path of spiritual progress, the keener his perception of the inner urge of aspiration, and the livelier his feeling of the impact of higher planes of consciousness.

Is Man the Limit of Evolution?

We have now an idea of the forces which are at work behind the emergence of qualitative differences in the material world. The question that next arises is: Are we to suppose that the evolutionary process has reached its highest limit with the birth of human personality? Or that man is the crowning consummation of evolution? Is it a fact that the only direction in which further progress lies would be in carrying to the utmost limit of development the latent capacities of the mind and in an increasing realization of man's moral and social ideals?

Such a supposition would involve a complete misreading of the fundamental trend of evolution. There are numerous indications in the human mind which point beyond the limited mentality and underscore the necessity of mind's self-completion beyond itself. It is notorious that mind, left to its own resources, can never reconcile its own paradoxes or self-discrepancies. It suffers from a radical division within itself, such as the conscious and the unconscious. It is torn by such conflicts as passion and reason, ego and nonego, etc. Such basic divisions and conflicts can be solved only by going beyond the limits of the mind and attaining a higher level of consciousness. To suggest that man as the mental being is the crown of evolution or the measure of things, is like the fabled frog-in-the-well imagining that the ocean might be just another well.

It may be argued that even though man may not be the last word of evolution, he himself is not capable of developing into a higher form of existence, such as the Superman. In that case, Supermanhood can hardly be presented as man's own ideal of self-perfection. The Superman would rather belong to a separate and independent level of creation. Taking for granted that there is likely to be an evolutionary leap or saltus from man to the Superman, that would not be a case of man himself getting transformed into the Superman, but just a case of nature by-passing the human level to lay the foundation for a totally different level of creation.

It is indeed true that that has hitherto been the character of nature's evolutionary leap. Nature bypassed the plant in creating the animal. She by-passed the animal in creating the human species. So also it might not be altogether unreasonable to infer that nature would perhaps one day bypass man in creating the next higher species of Superman. Moreover, every great type or pattern of being, answers to a peculiar form of delight of the creative energy. "Each form and way of being has its own appropriate way of the delight of being." Like all other beings, man too "has his own native law, limits, special kind of existence, *swabhāva, swadharma*; within these limits, he can extend and develop, but he cannot go outside them. If there is a perfection to which he has to arrive, it must be a perfection in his own kind, within his own law of being—the full play of it, but by observation of its mode and measure, not by transcendence."[3]

Now, it must be observed by way of criticism that though every pattern of living answers to a peculiar form of delight of being, that is no argument against the possibility that the creative delight includes also the joy of gradual working out of a truth inherent in Being. The cosmic plan includes no doubt the preservation of various types or patterns, but that does not surely preclude the joy of *growing into* a higher pattern by exceeding the limits of the lower.

"A drama without denouement may be an artistic possibility . . . (and) the drama of the earth-evolution might conceivably be of that character, but an intended or inherently predetermined denouement is also and more convincingly possible.[4] True, the plant itself did not develop or get transformed into the animal, nor did the animal itself develop or get transformed into man. Nature by-passed the animal in creating man. That is because the plant and the animal are in the nature of unconscious vehicles of the evolutionary urge. They are obviously incapable of conscious cooperation with the inherent purpose of evolution.

But the case is entirely different with man. Nature has come to attain self-consciousness in him. The impulse of self-exceeding seems to be an essential part of the law of self-development of man. The means for a conscious transition seems to be provided for among his unique spiritual powers. "Man has seen that there can be a higher status of consciousness than his own; the evolutionary oestrus is there in his parts of life and mind, the aspiration to ex-

---

[3] Sri Aurobindo, *The Life Divine*, p. 990.
[4] Ibid., p. 995.

ceed himself is delivered and articulate within him. . . . In him, then, the substitution of a conscious for a sub-conscious evolution has become conceivable and practicable, and it may well be concluded that the aspiration, the urge, the persistent endeavor immanent is a sure sign of Nature's will for a higher way to fulfillment, the emergence of a greater status."[5]

So, the objections to the possibility of man's self-growth into a higher pattern of being are quite unfounded. This is not, however, to suggest that the whole human race is likely one day to rise in a block to the supermental level. The human mental status will perhaps always, or at least for a very long period of time, be there, but it will be there not as an unsurpassable type or pattern, but as an open step towards the spiritual and supermental status.

The Vision of Supermanhood

The foregoing account of the nature and scope of evolution brings us to a vision of supermanhood as the next higher possibility of terrestrial evolution. There have been glimpses almost in all religions of a divine fulfillment of the human aspiration. In Christianity there has been the dream of a Kingdom of Heaven, or of a reign of the Saints on earth. Similarly, in Hinduism, we have the vision of a new *Satya Yuga,* or Kingdom of Truth emerging out of the ruins of destruction of the Iron age.

True, there are people who believe that heaven is heaven and earth is earth, and that "the twain shall never meet." They imagine an essential incompatibility between heaven and earth—between the glories of spiritual realization and the conditions of embodied existence in material circumstances—so that though the possibility of the emancipation of the human soul from its bondage on earth into a heavenly region of infinite knowledge and bliss is admitted, the descending of heaven on earth or a transformation of earth into heaven, is strenuously combated. But

---

[5] Ibid., p. 1005.

it has been our contention in the foregoing pages that the possibility of a divine transformation of human existence, or of the conscious evolution of man into Superman, is not only perfectly reasonable, but the secret and sovereign purpose of terrestrial evolution. The emergence of reason in the course of evolution made it possible for man to appear on earth. Through man's conscious cooperation with the creative force of evolution, the higher power of supermind may be called into overt operation in human life and society. The emergence of the supermind would transform man into Superman. It would effectuate a radical transformation of man's collective consciousness. It would lay the foundation for a unique world order governed by the forces of love, peace and progress.

The vision of supermanhood gives a definite shape to the popular idea of the Kingdom of Heaven on earth, and places it on the firm footing of philosophical reasoning. Just as life was previously latent in matter, making its appearance at a subsequent date in the course of evolution, and just as mind was previously latent in life, making its appearance at a subsequent date in the course of evolution, so also supermind which is now latent and secretly operative in our human mentality, is destined one day to be brought forth into explicit operation in the fullness of time. The complete unveiling of the Spirit in material conditions by means of the supermind is indeed the ultimate goal of terrestrial evolution.

Chapter 11

THE PRINCIPLE OF INDIVIDUALITY

The fundamental affirmation of nondualism is that the individual self (Ātman) is existentially identical with the Absolute. It is Being in its individualized mode of self-expression.

In its transcendental aspect, Being is the nontemporal root of all that is. It is the indeterminable ground of all existence. In its universal aspect, Being is cosmic creative energy. It is the all-originating, all-sustaining, all-consummating reality. Integral nondualism holds that the individual in its inmost essence is a unique focus of the nontemporal. It is an active center of the cosmic creative energy. In existence, it is identical with the Absolute. In form and function, it is different from the Absolute. In respect of both this identity and difference, individuality is a very real and significant component of Being.

The individual self is not a mere abstract power of the Absolute. Nor is it an unrecognizable element in the life of the Absolute. Nor is it a self-subsistent member of the Absolute conceived as a Republic of Selves. As a unique focus of the Absolute, the individual is essentially identical therewith, and therefore it contains within itself the seed of perfection and freedom.

The individual in his wholeness is not to be equated with the mind-body complex with which he is normally identified in his empirical life. There is a depth-dimension of human personality. Nonmental and transpersonal factors are present in the depth-dimension of being. The individual is also not to be equated with the ego principle which is an organizing principle of man's conscious experiences. The ego is the principle of exclusive particularity. It is that which separates an individual from other beings. The nonpersonal factor in him is that which unites him with the universal and the eternal without abrogating his individuality.

The purpose of this chapter is to make a comparative and critical study of some important theories concerning the principle of individuality. The elements of truth in those theories are duly acknowledged and harmoniously blended in the integral view of the individual.

The Monadic Theory

While discussing the problem of individuality, one is confronted at the very outset with what has been called the monadic theory of the individual. Monadism is the result of the application of the principle of atomism to the realm of spirit. It is inspired by the assumption that the ultimate constituents of the world are an infinite number of simple, indivisible, independent and self-contained units.

Leibnitz says that the really simple or indivisible unit must be non-extended, immaterial, or spiritual in character; because whatever is material is extended in space and whatever is extended is divisible. It is such immaterial constituents of the world—spiritual atoms or monads—which provide, in his view, true instances of individuality. The monadic theory is an extreme logical sequel to the conception of the individual as an exclusive particular. Ordinarily, the term 'individual' is used to signify an entity which has an independent existence and a distinctive character of its own, so that it can easily be distinguished from the rest of the world. The individual thus conceived as an exclusive particular or repellent unit is affirmed by monadism to be the only thing concretely real and substantial. Leibnitz holds that the individual monad or soul is substantial insofar as it is independent in respect of its action. It is an active force (*vis activa*), and it pursues its independent line of action entirely uninfluenced by any external agency. Individual souls are, in his view, "windowless." They do not receive any influence from without, nor do they exert any influence upon others. They are individual insofar as they combine exclusive particularity with substantiality.

In the case of the human individual, the monadic theory is reinforced by ethical considerations. The human individual is manifestly capable of free actions which are expressions of his own unique nature. He acts out of his own spontaneity, and owns responsibility for his actions. Mr. Howison contends that the human individual conceived as a moral personality is lifted above the sphere of efficient causality. He can by no stretch of imagination be said to be derived from antecedent factors, and fashioned *ab extra*. He is, in respect of his spiritual nature, self-molding and self-made. He refuses to be coerced, and is opened only to persuasion. He cannot be molded even by the superior power of God, unless and until he identifies himself with that power and thus makes it his own. It has been rightly observed that even God has to wait outside and knock on the doors of the heart of man. This leads Prof. Howison to develop his spiritualistic pluralism which treats human spirits as ontologically underived or as existents in their own right.

But the spiritualistic pluralism of both Leibnitz and Howison founders upon the inescapable fact of the interrelation and interdependence of the individual components of the universe. Individuals cannot be interrelated unless they are members of one system. And they can be members of one inclusive system only as modes of manifestation of the principle of totality that informs the system. That is why both Leibnitz and Howison feel constrained in the end to qualify their individualism with some principle of "ideal harmony". Leibnitz speaks of finite souls or monads as "fulgurations" of one Supreme Monad, the *Monus Monadum*. And Howison constantly refers the finite self to the Divine Center which is, in his view, the final cause of their development.

Individualism is, however, carried to its furthest logical extreme at the hands of Dr. McTaggart. If the individual is to maintain his character as a self-subsistent entity, he cannot be existentially subordinate to any central presiding self or a *Primus inter pares*. McTaggart holds that a self that enjoys being-for-self cannot be imagined to exist as part of the existence of another self. Likewise, whatever is part of the existence of a universal self must be a psychological content of that self—its perception or idea or feeling. Consequently, it cannot itself enjoy selfhood. Once you posit the existence of a Universal Self which is capable of comprehending within its being other selves, you feel logically constrained to exalt it into the all-engulfing Absolute. The admission of the Absolute Self amounts to a reduction of all finite spirits to mere modes of consciousness of the Absolute. The finite self can hardly maintain its selfhood consistent with its inclusion in the existence of one all-embracing Spirit. So McTaggart affirms that the individual selves are, in their deepest essence, eternally self-subsistent. To use his terminology, individual selves are "primary parts" of the Universe.[1]

But even though individual selves are self-subsistent, according to McTaggart they are certainly not self-enclosed. They exist not in isolation, but in harmonious association with one another. They are not shut up within the enclosure of their detached personality, living out an insular existence of their own, strong in solid singleness like Lucretian atoms. The assumption of isolated existence of individual selves violently clashes with the patent facts of spiritual communion and social interdependence. Individuals are in point of truth interrelated members of an organic or superorganic system. McTaggart conceives of this system as the impersonal unity of a society or a college. This unity is sustained, not by the all-engulfing consciousness of any universal self, but by the relations of love and perfect mutual understanding in which the plurality of selves stand to one another. The logical sequal

[1] John McTaggart, *The Nature of Existence*, Vol. II, p. 120.

to the basic assumptions of McTaggart is that individual selves are beginningless and endless in their self-subsistence, and that they are underived and imperishable, which conclusion McTaggart boldly faces. If empirical facts appear to run counter to this conclusion, a little metaphysical distinction would be enough to remove that difficulty. McTaggart maintains that it is only *sub specie temporis* that individual selves appear to be gradually progressing towards an ideal perfection. *Sub specie aeternitatis* they are in actual possession of eternal perfection. In other words, empirical selves are manifestations in time of transcendent selves who enjoy timeless perfection.

Individualism is not only the outcome of certain logical and ethical considerations, but has also the support of a particular type of spiritual experience. It is in reliance upon a profound spiritual realization that the Sānkhya School of Indian philosophy declares that the individual spirits (purusas) are, in respect of their intrinsic nature, eternally perfect and beyond birth and death, growth and decay. The individual self is, according to the Sānkhya, in the nature of pure, unobjective consciousness, eternally placed above the ephemeral joys and sorrows of worldly life. The empirical self which is its manifestation in time is an organization of the elements of nature (Prakṛti), a physical-vital-mental complex, which is penetrated by the light of pure consciousness. It is this empirical self which has to struggle through the various colorful experiences of birth, death and rebirth. In all its struggles and thrilling adventures in the cosmic drama, the empirical self is, however, sustained by that unique transcendent self whose shadow or empirical counterpart it is. The multiplicity of empirical selves is not an illusion, but a reflection of the real multiplicity of transcendent selves.

The unity of our world of experience is traceable, according to the Sānkhya, not to the nondualism of one ultimate Self, but to the identity of one common Nature (Prakṛti). It is because Nature is one common stuff of our experience that the universe presents the appearance of being one all-embracing whole. But that does not destroy the manifoldness of the individual self. The Sānkhya contends that there is an overwhelming mass of empirical evidence in support of the doctrine of plurality of selves, which evidence is provided by the scheme of bondage and liberation (*bandhamoksa-vyāvasthā*) and the scheme of pleasure and pain (*sukha-duḥkha-vyāvasthā*). The liberation of one individual does not mean the liberation of other individuals, and the joys and sorrows of one individual are entirely different from those of others.

The Sānkhya position has however been criticized on the ground that the schemes of liberation and bondage, and pleasure and pain, can pretty well be explained on the basis of wide differences among empirical selves. It is unnecessary for their explanation to carry the element of differentiation to the transcendent spiritual reality. Different individuals are happy or miserable, elated or depressed, according to their identification with different bodies and their involvement in different social situations. Such differences are no proof of any real division within the life of the pure spirit. Moreover the Sānkhya thinkers fail to supply any principle of differentiation which would mark off one transcendent self from another. The pure undifferentiated consciousness which is affirmed to be the essence of the self can admit of no differentiation or plurality except by associatism with the divisions of matter. So, the Vedānta points out that the self which is in its inmost essence pure consciousness, must needs be like one infinite space, undivided and indivisible. The plurality of selves are real only from the empirical standpoint of ignorance. They are like artificially created divisions within one infinite space.

The Modal or Adjectival Theory

The theory of the individual as a self-subsistent exclusive entity is rejected by those who take their stand upon the fundamental unity of all existence. Spinoza conceives of reality as one infinite substance such as embraces all finite existents within itself. This is true of spiritual as well as of material things. Human personalities, dependent as they are upon the one infinite personality we call God, can hardly be treated as "substances," because independent existence is, according to Spinoza, of the very essence of substantiality.

Spinoza therefore looks upon individuals as mere modes or modifications of one ultimate Reality. In respect of their spiritual nature, they are modes of the infinite consciousness of God. In respect of their physical existence, they are modes of the infinite extension of God. Human beings who are mind-body complexes, are modifications of God who is self-conscious and self-extended. As such, they do not enjoy real freedom of will and initiative of action. God is entirely immanent in them. And all the thoughts and actions of men are finally to be explained in terms of the Divine immanence. Their appearance of substantiality and freedom owes itself to the isolating standpoints of sensuous imagination. All talk of self-contained existence and detached spontaneity is in fact but meaningless verbiage.

The pantheistic doctrine of finite individuality as a mere mode of appearance is strongly reinforced by the dialectic of absolutism. Whereas Spinoza denies the substantiality of the human individual on the ground that he is not independent in existence, Bradley and Bosanquet repudiate his reality on the ground that he is shot through and through with logical contradictions. Immediately one starts examining the nature of the individual self, one is confronted with a swelling mass of self-discrepancies. The self provides no satisfactory principle of uniting the one and the many. Bradley points out that like all other finite things it can be said in regard to the self also that its nature or "what" travels beyond the limits of its existence or "that" inasmuch as it depends for its nature upon the relation to other selves and objects. The self is said to be infected by the relations in which it stands with the rest of the universe; "external relations enter its essence and so ruin its independency."[2] It passes one's understanding how the variety of its functions, states and objects can be brought into harmonious union with its oneness and simplicity.

What is the relation in which the identical and permanent self may be said to stand to the changing diversity of psychical contents? If the relation in question be a vital and essential one, then one fails to comprehend how the self can maintain its identity or unity. If on the contrary the relation be a non-essential one—if, that is to say, the self stands alone from the psychic plurality, either having no character of its own or a character unknown and unknowable—then it may be a fine thing in itself, but it would be sheer mockery to call it the self of a man.[3] True, the self is somehow experienced by us as a principle of unity in diversity, but so long as the principle cannot be made self-coherent to rational comprehension, it cannot be affirmed to be real in the form in which we experience it. So far as it is known and comprehended, the self proclaims its unreality by betraying self-discrepancies within itself. But still, though the self is not an ultimately real form, it is, according to Bradley, the highest form of experience we possess. It is a concept immensely helpful in organizing systematically the manifold experiences of an individual.

The modal or adjectival theory of the finite individual has a most vigorous and eloquent advocate in Dr. Bosanquet. He holds that the Absolute is the one true individual reality, and that finite individuals are "in ultimate analysis connections of content within the real Individual to which they belong"[4] and of which they are "ultimately predicates." This follows from the view that individuality means systematic character, of which self-coherence and comprehensiveness are two inseparable aspects. As finitude

---

[2] F. H. Bradley, *Appearance and Reality,* p. 103.

[3] Ibid., p. 74.

[4] Bernard Bosanquet, *Logic* Vol. II (London: Oxford University Press, 1911), p. 258.

is by its very nature the seat of self-discrepancy, the Absolute is the only perfect embodiment of the principle of individuality, for the Absolute alone is a perfect system. It is the most self-coherent as well as most comprehensive unity of all experiences. A finite individual is "here and now beyond escape, an element in the Absolute," and can by no means be treated as a self-subsistent member thereof. Although he occupies a unique position in the realm of appearance, still he cannot escape the common fate of an all-pervasive transfusion in taking his place in the Absolute.

The individual self is no doubt the highest embodiment directly known to us of the principle of totality. The unique function of finite individuality is that it is the living copula between the Absolute and external Nature. Every self is a representative center of the external world; some portion of Nature "comes alive" in it. It is an empty principle of totality having no prior content or organization of its own. "All finite minds focus and draw their detail from some particular sphere of external nature."[5] "The spiritual individual," says Bosanquet, "has no separately distinguishable nucleus; he is the utterance of his place and time, a sub-variant of the content of his age, and a derivative of his family stock, like a bead on a plant." He is the appearance at a certain stage of an omnipotent principle, which elicits its whole definite content and development from its surroundings.

Nature or the realm of externality lives in the lives of conscious beings. All conscious beings also live in and through nature. "The self which makes the environment is itself all soaked in environment." The Absolute is the "perfect union of mind and nature, absorbing the world of nature by and through the world of selves."[6]

It is "the totality of a hold on reality which permeates in its degree all the conscious creatures of the creation,

---

[5] Bernard Bosanquet, *The Principle of Individuality and Value,* op. cit., p. 371.
[6] Ibid., p. 382.

and uses all its externality.''[7] The Absolute lays hold of
external nature by and through finite selves, just as the
mind of a great dramatist lays hold of certain portions of
the external through the characters of his drama.

The view that finite individuality is after all a vanishing quantity has also the backing of a particular type of
spiritual experience. There is a level of spiritual realization in which individuality appears to be entirely liquidated. The mystic's *via negativa* or path of negation reveals the Spirit in its aspect of pure undifferentiated consciousness, or featureless unity. When the purified and
spiritualized intellect of man catches the reflection of that
featureless unity, he experiences a distinct loss of the sense
of separative existence. There is indeed a dissolution of
exclusive individuality on the attainment of liberation
from the bonds of Ignorance. Moreover, having attained
liberation, it is quite possible for the soul to choose to
remain, by an exercise of freedom, absorbed in the static
calm of unitary experience. The *advaitavāda* of Śaṅkara
and the *nirvāṇa-vāda* of Buddha build upon such transcendental spiritual experience. They look upon individuality as entirely a product of Ignorance.

Buddhism treats the individual as a continuous stream
of cognitions, which loses itself in the sea of ineffable
impersonal delight that *Nirvāṇa* is. *Advaitism* holds that
since individuality is a product of Ignorance it is no more
than an illusion, a fleeting phenomenon. It is therefore
as untenable to maintain that the Absolute is a synthetic
unity of finite selves as to suggest that the individual self
is a modification of the Absolute. It is more in accord
with the spirit of *Advaitism* to say that the individual self
is non-different from the Absolute than to say that they
are identical, because the notion of identity necessarily
presupposes some amount of difference. While for Bradley, the individual self is in the ultimate context a submerged element of the overruling harmony of the Absolute, according to Śaṅkara, the individual self is in respect

[7] Ibid., p. 382.

of individuality an eternally cancelled unreality and in respect of selfhood the eternally accomplished Absolute. The Śaṅkarite position is an extreme logical sequel to ascetic nondualism. It is also the outcome of an exclusive emphasis upon the transcendental mode of spiritual experience.

But if individuality be in the last analysis an unreality, then our life in the world must be void of ultimate significance. Individuality is the center of all actions and the support of all effort and initiative in the world. If the individual be only a passing appearance, then the entire stream of life, which is an unceasing stream of activity, must be reduced to a meaningless dream. To suggest that life begins with the appearance of individuality and aims at the dissolution of the same in the Supreme, is to reduce creation to a game of illusion. To affirm with Bradley that the individual self is an organ of imperfect and self-contradictory self-articulation of the Absolute is to admit that life and creation are in essence a cosmic blunder. It implies that the Absolute perpetually indulges in an absurd scheme of self-manifestation in terms of the relative and the finite—a scheme which is foredoomed to failure.

Chapter 12

THE INTEGRAL VIEW OF THE INDIVIDUAL

All theories which affirm the unreality of the individual are vitiated by a confusion between the true individual and the exclusive particular or between the individual self and the ego. True, in the crucible of pure spiritual experience exclusive particularity undergoes a process of dissolution. But such a dissolution hardly amounts to loss of authentic individuality. Freedom from the shackles of *māyā* or lower *prakṛti* undoubtedly implies the liquidation of the ego, but that is an essential condition for the discovery of the authentic individual self. True it is that on the attainment of liberation from the bonds of Ignorance, the individual self can choose freely either to fall quiescent in the static consciousness of the Supreme, or to go in for conscious cooperation with the evolutionary urge of the Supreme. But such exercise of freedom on the attainment of illumination is itself the strongest argument in support of the reality of the individual self. Even when the self chooses to merge itself in the fathomless depth of Being, the reality of self as free choice is demonstrated. The integral view of the individual reveals him as a real component of Being. Individuality is neither an unreal appearance nor a self-subsistent entity. It is a real and significant center of self-expression of Being. It is instrumental to the self-representation of Being in infinitely diverse forms. It is the agency by which ever new values are created.

Egocentric and Cosmocentric Individuality

A distinction of vital importance is that beween ego-centric individuality and cosmocentric individuality. The former is the product of ignorance, and therefore in a sense unreal. The latter is inspired by an understanding of the cosmic purpose of Being. When a person is domi-nated in his thinking and living by his exclusive self-interest, his individuality is egocentric. When a person discovers his ultimate ground of existence, his authentic individuality emerges. He begins to feel a spiritual kin-ship with the entire universe. He experiences a sense of responsibility for the entire living creation. His heart beats in unison with the all of existence. His soul is aflame with the spirit of dedication to cosmic welfare. In fine, he becomes cosmocentric. He understands how uniqueness and universality, I-ness and Thou-ness, are in-explicably interwoven in the concrete texture of his being.

What is liquidated on the attainment of spiritual libera-tion is the ego-centric individuality of an individual. Out of the ashes of the ego is reborn a new individual. His deepest potentiality as an active center of Being is dyna-mized. He learns to respond to the world in its wholeness by virtue of this inner realization of the wholeness of Being.

The individual in his individualized form is neither an illusory appearance nor a self-contained substance. Nothing in the world is absolutely self-contained. Self-subsistent individuality exists only as an abstraction in the mind of the supreme egotist. Everything real in the world lives in constant interaction and interdependence with the rest of the world. It is a link in the vast system of interrelationships that the universe is. Each is in all and all is in each. Every individual, therefore, is essentially a unique and specific configuration of the elements of universal energy. He is a specific constellation of the space-time continuum, endowed with some emergent powers and qualities.

Freedom and Self-Existence

The most prerogative feature of the human individual is this potential for freedom and self-existence. But even in his case, existence does not mean self-contained being or absolutely isolated being, cut off from the rest of the universe. Absolutely isolated existence is the path of perdition, not of self-realization. The authentic self is the individual as related in his wholeness to the Whole. Selfhood is the integrated wholeness of being of the individual, not the subsistence of a detached entity. Every self is a unique way of mirroring the universe, not a way of negating it.

So, true self-existence means one's ability to live in the world out of the depth of one's own being. The ability to relate one's self to the world in the light of one's inner vision of truth. The ability to cultivate the best within one's self and offer one's best to the world in one's own freely chosen manner.

True freedom is indeed an attribute of man's self consciousness. It does not mean absence of all determination. Absolute indeterminism is a myth of wishful thinking. It is a figment of undisciplined imagination. Authentic freedom inherent in human individuality is the ability to transcend all fixed determinations. The animal is determined by his instinct. By virtue of his reason and his imagination of boundless possibility man can transcend the determinism of instinct. He can allow his conduct to be determined by his awareness of ever new principles and values. Man is essentially a rule-making creature. He is always breaking past rules and forging new ones. His mind is always exploring new possibilities of self-development and self-expression. His evolution is marked by ever-changing modes of self-determination.

A conservative chooses to be determined by some well-established and time-tested laws of society. A liberal wants to modify established laws in recognition of changing times. He is willing to accept time as an essential determinant of human conduct.

An orthodox religious person is well satisfied with the established religious authority as the determinant of his religious conduct. A mystic considers that to be a subtle form of bondage. He wishes to break the bonds of authoritarian religion. But in doing so he is willing to move into another form of self-determination. He allows his whole life to be determined by the will of God as revealed to his inward consciousness.

Uniqueness, Relatedness, and Transcendence

Individuality is in its essence, as Sri Aurobindo puts it, a poise of being of the Absolute. As a particular existent, every individual has his aspect of uniqueness. He is a focalized expression of the universe. He represents a special and peculiar combination of talents and limitations, potentialities and dispositions.

But he has also his aspect of relatedness—relatedness to the whole. He hungers for the whole. The spirit of the whole is dynamically present at the center of his being. He wishes to complete himself by association with others. He wishes also to make himself whole by harmonizing the diverse elements of his own nature—by integrating his instincts, emotions, thoughts and insights. Characteristic of the individual psyche is its integrative power, its self-healing and whole-making ability.

The indwelling presence of the whole or the absolute in the individual also generates a self-transcending urge. Consequently, no individual is satisfied with his given actuality, with his "is-ness." He is always reaching out for something higher and greater. He is always trying to overcome himself. He is always projecting himself into the future in pursuit of ever-new values.

This self-transcending impulse may assume social, cultural, or pure spiritual forms. Culturally, an individual sacrifices himself at the altar of some such cultural value as scientific pursuit, aesthetic creation, philosophic integration, etc. Socially, he transcends himself by subordinating his private self-interest to the larger interests of the family, community, nation, political party, humanity, etc. Spiritually, he transcends himself by an act of total self-offering to the Divine. He allows all other interests and pursuits of life to be submerged in his one overmastering impulse to fathom the mystery of Being and to live in union with Being.

Socio-moral transcendence reaches ultimate fulfillment in the spirit of universal love and compassion. Cultural self-transcendence reaches fulfillment in the spirit of dedication to some cultural value. Spiritual self-transcendence reaches ultimate fulfillment in the discovery of one's absolute relationship to the Absolute. In the balanced growth of an individual the social, ethical, cultural and spiritual aspects of personality have to be harmoniously fulfilled.

Self-Integration

An integrated individual is one who becomes aware of his rootedness in the Supreme. Therein lies the essence of his enlightenment and freedom. He breaks the bonds of ignorance and egotism in all forms. But since the world is the diversified expression of the Supreme, the enlightened person necessarily experiences a vivid feeling of oneness with the world. Genuine wisdom cannot but produce the spirit of universal love. The experience of wisdom and love enables an individual to function at his best in the service of God and man.

Wisdom transcends individuality. The wise man lives as a unique focus of pure Transcendence. He is freed from the fetters of the ego. He conquers fear and anxiety, doubt and despair. He is united with the depth of his being. So, the Muṇḍaka Upaniṣad says, "When a person beholds the Supreme, his knot of the heart is cut and all doubts are dispelled."[1]

---

[1] Muṇḍaka Upaniṣad, II, 2.9.

Love universalizes individuality. The individual who experiences the love that flows from wisdom knows how to sacrifice all personal comfort for the sake of others.

Creativity intensifies individuality. The individual of light and love knows how to mobilize the resources of his personality in creating new values. Guided by his vision of truth and spirit of love, he offers his best for the good of others. With a profound stirring of the soul, there is a free and spontaneous release of psychic energy in meaningful self-expression.

Love is the way of self-expansion. It is the flame that consumes the particularity of an individual and fills the world with his universal essence. It is the way of the candle which burns itself while filling the whole room with its light. It is the way of the flower which withers away while filling the environment with its charm and fragrance. It is the way of the star which explodes while dispelling the darkness of the night.

Chapter 13

THE LONGING FOR IMMORTALITY

The desire for immortality has been throughout history a powerful motivation of human conduct. It has inspired the noblest and most daring of human deeds. Man has embraced death with a smiling face with a view to conquering death. He has accepted extinction in one form in order to gain imperishable glory in another form. He has sacrificed life evanescent in order to gain life everlasting. The longing for immortality has indeed expressed itself in various ways.

Immortality is essentially an attribute of consciousness. It is an attribute of wisdom, love and dedication to higher values. By boldly looking death in the face, man overcomes death. By realizing the fundamental truth about life and death, he goes beyond life and death. By perceiving his eternal relationship to the Supreme, he participates in the life eternal of the Supreme. By gaining insight into the mystery of time, he is lifted out of the perishing moments of time.

By virtue of his identification with higher values and in proportion to his fulfillment of them in life, man appropriates the imperishable property of higher values.

Finally, man attains immortality by achieving integration of personality, and by probing into the non-temporal dimension of his being. A thoroughly integrated person becomes fearless because he discovers his rootedness in the eternal.

Let us see in what different ways down through the ages man's basic longing for immortality has sought fulfillment.

Social Immortality

First of all, the passion for immortality seeks fulfillment in society. It may assume the form of desire for children—for bright and illustrious children. Through the uninterrupted continuation of progeny, a person gains a sense of immortality. His name is immortalized in the annals of the family tree.

The longing for immortality may also assume the form of leaving some creditable achievement for succeeding generations to admire. Ancient rulers of Egypt used to create pyramids. The great emperor, Sajahan wanted to immortalize his wife by creating the magnificent Taj Mahal. By immortalizing his beloved wife he also secretly desired to immortalize himself. Creative thinkers, poets, painters, etc. attain immortality by leaving behind them immortal works of artistic creation. Social workers achieve immortality by pouring out their life blood in building some great social institution, such as a school, a hospital, a research institute, a church, etc. Martyrs gain immortality by giving their lives for a noble cause. Politicians seek immortality through self-identification with the prosperity and the glory of the mother land. Humanitarians identify themselves with the survival, welfare and progress of the human race.

Idealistic Immortality

The longing for immortality may seek fulfillment through the contemplation and realization of timeless ideas, forms, or values. When that happens, immortality assumes the pure idealistic form.

An artist beholds the enchanting form of beauty in a little flower or in a charming landscape. In contemplating the timeless essence of beauty he feels lifted above the realm of perishable things. He has a feeling of participation in its nontemporal being. His own existence is merged in it, through contemplative oneness. He may feel that now that he is one with the immortal form of beauty, it does not matter if he dies as a particular physical entity.

Similarly, a scientist may be searching for truth in a particular sphere of nature. He has a sense of dedication to truth and identification with truth. Once in a while, he catches a glimpse of the truth he is trying to articulate and establish. By virtue of his vision of truth, he participates in truth's nontemporal being. At the exalted moment of his truth-vision, he experiences immortality. He feels lifted out of the realm of death into the imperishable abode of light and knowledge. His inner being is suffused with the profound joy of communion with truth.

Let us now sum up the foregoing. Social immortality consists in one's feeling of oneness with the society—with its survival, welfare, and progress. By virtue of devotion to a noble social cause, the individual dies to live in the advance of society. Idealistic immortality consists in one's dynamic self-identification with some cultural values, such as scientific pursuit, aesthetic creation, ethical perfection. etc. It is unitive contemplation of the timeless essence of some great Idea.

Personal Immortality

It should, however, be observed here that man's longing for immortality is not completely satisfied in terms of social, cultural, or idealistic immortality. The average human being secretly desires for the immortality of his own individual existence as a unique and distinct person. This may be called personal immortality. If the ostensible facts of experience do not lend support to personal immortality, his creative imagination proceeds to fulfill this irrepressible psychic need in sublimated forms.

Broadly speaking, there are two types of people. They are, to use the words of William James, the tough-minded and the tender-minded. The tough-minded people are hard boiled, realistic and extroverted. They are willing to adjust themselves to the harsh realities of life. They are satisfied with socio-cultural immortality, that is, the immortality of some great achievement in social or cultural fields.

But those who are tender-minded secretly wish for the prolongation of their own personal, individualized existence. It is not enough for them to leave at death a legacy of creative action. In order that life may make sense, one must also individually continue to live after death in some form or other. A valuable social or cultural achievement would, for the tender-minded, lose its value if it cannot contribute to the author's prolongation of life beyond the grave. If the facts of actual experience—the facts of common sense, science and self-realization—do not lend support to the idea of indefinite, personal immortality, the miracle of faith must be invoked to fulfill one's irrepressible psychic need for it.

So, the notion of personal immortality—the indefinite prolongation of the individual after death—plays a dominant role in popular religion and theology. It assumes various forms.

Some visualize personal immortality in terms of bodily resurrection. It is considered possible for the virtuous and the faithful to rise from tombs one day and make a triumphal entry into the supernatural Kingdom of Heaven in order to enjoy the immortal company of the merciful Godhead.

If and when it is realized that the gross physical body is not an indispensable component of an individual human being's spiritual existence, the idea of disembodied immortality on higher spiritual planes gains prominence. A virtuous and faithful person goes back to the paradise from which he had a fall on account of his sinful defiance of divine authority. He acquires a new celestial body. It is made of subtle, supernatural substance. It enables him to participate in the indescribable glory and supernatural delight of at-one-ment with the Heavenly Father in paradise. Thus, the Christian idea of paradise regained through atonement with the Father in Heaven arises.

The above may be called the supernaturalistic theory of immortality. Supernatural immortality may be static or dynamic. Some people conceive of supernatural immortality in terms of eternal rest and supernal peace in heaven. It is the ecstatic joy of a renewed existence in the kingdom of heaven which is the realm of perfection. But some people—those who are especially ethically-minded—conceive of supernatural immortality in terms of unceasing progress. It is a kind of asymptotic approximation to the infinite goal of perfection. In its upward journey the soul passes through higher and higher levels of consciousness, through the ever-expanding splendors of the Infinite Spirit. Different ideas of supernatural immortality reflect different types of emotional urge of the human psyche. *Vaiṣṇava* supernaturalism in India has elaborately dealt with different types of supernatural self-fulfilment.

Some spiritual seekers wish to dwell in the same lofty plane of existence as that of God (*sālokya*). Some wish to acquire the same form as that of God (*sārūpya*). Some wish to acquire the same law of action as that of God (*sādharmya*). Some wish to acquire the same supernatural powers, or the ability to work miracles such as belong to God (*sārṣti*). Some wish to enter into the celestial body of God and get merged in His blissful and universal substance, (*sāyujya*). Some wish to serve God unconditionally, having set aside all personal desires including even the desire for salvation or liberation (*sevā*). The Bengal School of *Vaiṣṇavism* holds that the spirit of unconditional surrender and service is the loftiest spiritual ideal. Even the notion of salvation appears egotistic when compared with this idea of divine service, regardless of all personal considerations, such as sin and salvation.

But, it should be noted here that behind the willingness to renounce even the desire for liberation, the desire to serve God as a definite individual entity persists. Such a desire to serve God with utmost self-surrender is very commendable so long as one is alive. But when such a desire is projected beyond death, seeking fulfillment in some supernatural realm, the Vedāntic criticism that this also is a product of ignorance becomes very pertinent. From the standpoint of supreme wisdom the notions of a personal God, the supernatural region, the desire for personal immortality, even though such personal immortality is visualized in terms of utmost surrender to the Deity—all this belongs in the realm of *māyā*.

But, the ideal of selfless service of the Supreme here and now in this very world is an element of permanent value in *Vaiṣṇava* mysticism. Let us illustrate this ideal with the aid of an ancient anecdote.

One time the great sage Nārada went to have a visit with the Lord Kṛṣṇa in his heavenly abode. On hearing that Kṛṣṇa had a little headache, Nārada was eager to help in whatever way he could. Kṛṣṇa suggested that a little dust taken from the feet of a perfect devotee might cure him of his headache. Nārada thought that such a therapeutic item must be easy enough to obtain. Because, was not the whole world full of Kṛṣṇa's devotees?

He first went to some well-known ascetics and yogis. But all of them were shocked to hear the purpose of Nārada's visit. How could they allow a particle of dust from their feet to be applied to the great lord Kṛṣṇa's forehead? Would not that amount to a great act of sinfulness on their part? So, they thought that the whole thing was either a big joke, or a devil's trap.

Nārada now realized the gravity of the situation and the difficulty of his undertaking. So, he now proceeded to Sri Kṛṣṇa's wife, Rukmini Devi. But no sooner had she learned of the purpose of Nārada's visit than she bit her tongue in shame. The Hindu wife's proper place is at the feet of her lord. How can dust from her feet be applied to the husband's forehead? That would indeed be an unthinkable sin. And a shameless violation of social decorum.

Disappointed and disillusioned, Nārada went to Sri Kṛṣṇa to report the whole matter. Kṛṣṇa smiled. He then recommended the final solution to the problem. He told

Nārada to go to the remote and obscure village of Vṛndā-van and seek the cooperation of his humble devotee, Sri Rādhā. Traveling a long distance, Nārada went to Rādhā and told her everything. Now, Rādhā's first reaction was that she was not probably the right kind of devotee who could be of real help to her Lord. Who was she, after all, when there were so many world-famous ascetics, yogis, mystics and philosophers? But Nārada assured her that in Kṛṣṇa's own estimation she was an authentic devotee. At that, Rādhā was delighted. She said, "Nārada, take this dust from my feet and go to Kṛṣṇa's place as fast as you can. He must be relieved of his headache at the earliest opportunity. This may be an act of sinfulness, a violation of ethical code and social decorum on my part. It may cost me my salvation and my place in heaven. But when Kṛṣṇa is in trouble, nothing matters. The happiness of my Lord is my only concern."

According to the Bengal School of *Vaiṣṇavism*, uncondi-tional service of the Lord (*sevā*) is the very essence of love and devotion. Love is total self-giving to the Divine. The only concern of love is to be ready to serve the be-loved in a spirit of total dedication. Considerations of personal sin and suffering fade into insignificance before the joy of divine service. By virtue of such self-effacing love, the devotee is most intimately united with the Divine after death in the supernatural kingdom of heaven.

Chapter 14

IMMORTALITY AS ESSENCE OF THE SPIRIT

According to the teaching of the Upaniṣads, all men are in essence "children of immortality."[1] They are modes of manifestation of the Eternal, just as waves are modes of manifestation of the ocean. Or, just as finite spaces are modes of manifestation of the one, undivided, and indivisible space. Men as finite spirits are modes of manifestation of the one, undivided and indivisible ocean of consciousness.

Immortality is, according to the Upaniṣads, the very birthright of man. It is his divine heritage. It is within his power to lift the veil of ignorance and consciously realize the heritage of immortality.

The Democratic Theory of Immortality

Since all men are essentially children of immortality, they are all destined sooner or later to attain immortality. Since immortality is immanent in the spiritual essence of man, as soon as he realizes the essential structure of his being, he attains life eternal. This may be called the democratic theory of immortality. It is a rejection of the doctrine of eternal damnation. No soul can be totally lost, because every soul is essentially a focus of the eternal. Every soul represents a unique value, and so it is eternally preserved in the bosom of the Infinite.

The concept of universal salvation is based upon both ontological and religious grounds. Ontologically, every

---

[1] *Amṛtasya putrāḥ. See Śvetāśvatara Upaniṣad, II. 5.*

individual self (Ātman), by virtue of its essential non-difference from the Eternal, is destined in the course of evolution to realize its union with the eternal. The growth of personality aims at the realization of what one essentially is.

Religiously speaking, universal salvation is guaranteed by the higher conception of God as absolute love. The notion of eternal damnation stems from the idea of God as ruthless justice. The ruling power of the world is conceived as relentless and vindictive, ready to torture individuals for the pitfalls of finitude over which they have little control. Religion evolves a higher conception of God when law is combined with love, justice is tempered with mercy. This found expression in the conception of God as absolute love (Buddha, Kṛṣṇa, Christ, etc.). It found expression in the idea of Viṣṇu as the loving ruler of the world. God as love preserves all values. In the scheme of the world there is no room either for Divine partiality and favoritism or for eternal punishment in the fires of hell. There is abundant and repeated opportunity for all individuals to realize the spiritual potential of their existence.

According to Vedānta, immortality in its ultimate spiritual significance is not the continuation of existence after death. Rather, it is essentially the light of awareness of the eternal that dwells at the center of one's being. The eternal is the very foundation of one's being. It is not to be identified either with the past or with the durational present or with the future. It is not to be construed as continued existence in time. It is in truth a mode of self-poise beyond time and its different periods, beyond life and death. In consequence, the eternal can be realized at any moment of time. One need not wait for it until after death. One can realize it here and now while living in the flesh.

According to Vedānta, immortality is a characteristic of authentic self-awareness. It is an attribute of spiritual enlightenment. The moment a person overcomes his self-alienation, and realizes his inmost self and his rootedness in the eternal, he partakes of immortality. When he experiences immortality, in a sense, nothing changes. There is just the awareness of things as they are, essentially and eternally. It is like a man desperately searching for his spectacles in every nook and corner of his room, and then suddenly finding out that they are already on his eyes. Or, it is like a poor orphan boy, suffering untold misery, one day coming to know that he is the heir to a large real estate which his deceased uncle left for him long ago. Now, this is only the discovery of what already is and what has been. It involves no change in the order of things and events. But, from another standpoint, everything changes. In the case of the poor orphan, it is a sudden and radical transition from poverty to opportunity, from despair to hope, from misery to happiness. There is a world of difference between ignorance and knowledge. A person who comes to know what Eternity is, suddenly experiences a complete transfiguration. He sloughs off the old skin and is reborn, as it were, in an entirely different world. He becomes one with the Eternal.

Let us imagine that a wave rolling upon the surface of the ocean begins one day to feel depressed about its despicable nothingness. It is surrounded on all sides by countless other waves clashing with one another and threatening to swallow it at any moment. It is afraid of being crushed at any time by the vast, infinite ocean. But, suddenly, a new insight unfolds in its mind. It need not be afraid of the tempestuous vastness of the ocean. For is it not an integral part of the ocean itself? Is it not the ocean itself in a particular mode of expression? The supreme joy of its individualized existence lies in playing with other waves to the tune of time. All the waves together make a total drama of music and movement on the bosom of the ocean. By virtue of the new insight, the wave immediately conquers its depression and despair; its previous feeling of nothingness and insignificance melts away. It begins to partake of the glory of the vast ocean. That does not mean it ceases to be a wave. Nor that it gets lost and dissolved in the ocean. On the contrary, enriched and delighted by the new insight, it enjoys the merriment of the wavy drama.

The wave was in depression so long as it was ignorant. It had the illusion of existential separation from the ocean and from the other waves. The moment the illusion is shattered, there is a sudden transformation of outlook. There is no more any blind clinging to its particular wave form. By virtue of oneness with the ocean, liberation is achieved from ignorant identification with the impermanent. The glory of each wave-form lies in running its full course with gracefulness and joy.

Immortality conceived as conscious realization of one's existential oneness with the eternal is known in Vedānta as *mokṣa*. It is emancipation from ignorance and self-alienation. Ignorance is separative consciousness. It produces the illusion that a person exists by himself like a Lucretian atom. He believes that he is separate from God and thus is sinful. That he is separate from fellow-beings and therefore can afford to ignore them or destroy them for his self-aggrandizement. On account of such separative consciousness, he desperately clings to his individualized form as the supreme value of life. Thus, ignorance leads to egotism or narcissistic concern. And, out of ignorance and egotism, there arises a bumper crop of fear and anxiety, greed and violence, hatred and hostility, etc. The light of truth alone can destroy such a poisonous crop of darkness. It is through crucifixion of the individualized form that the reality of the self can arise in its eternal glory.

But is not the human individual much more than a wave? Is there not a self-subsistent and permanent spiritual substance underlying all bodily and material change? Does not the Vedāntic view amount to a denial of the reality and substantiality of the human spirit? Is not man's freedom an attribute of his substantive reality?

These are issues of crucial importance indeed. In discussing them we have to set aside mere metaphors and analogies and examine the categories of thought involved in these questions.

The categories of substance and free-will, understood as supernatural or mystical entities, are only the relics of medieval metaphysics. In modern science, psychology and philosophy, such categories are rejected as exploded myths, as metempirical notions. In physical science, the notion of material substance has been replaced by the notion of energy, process, action. In psychology the notion of soul substance has been replaced by that of psychic energy or libido. In modern philosophy, the notion of metaphysical substance has been replaced by that of Being beyond substance and quality, cause and effect.

Let us explain this matter a little further. From the popular standpoint, there is an absolute distinction between a substance and a wave. There is also an absolute distinction between the free-will of man and a natural process. These distinctions are certainly valid. But it is time to realize that such distinctions are only relatively valid. They are not absolutely valid to the extent of implying fundamental, ontological divisions at the heart of reality. We are dealing here with qualitative differences characteristic of the different modes of expression of the same Being, not with separate ontological categories. We are dealing here with different standpoints, not with different realities. For instance, from the standpoint of eternity, even a mountain is nothing but a wave on the ocean of cosmic energy. The individual human soul, supposing it covers in its evolution a period of one million years, is also nothing but a wave of birth, growth, decay and death —or of life, death, rebirth and release—rolling on the ocean of timeless consciousness.

Similarly, the free choice or decision of a human individual certainly differs quantitatively from the blossoming of a flower. But is it not possible that even this distinction is only relatively valid? The free choice of a person is also in ultimate analysis a natural process of his psychical existence. It is a psychical process accompanied by the emergent quality of consciousness. It is a mental process animated by the consciousness of higher values. In subduing some lower impulse, it is still inspired (or determined) by some other impulse, say the impulse of devotion to some such value as truth, justice, perfection, etc.

In popular imagination, a rock and a wave are absolutely different ontological categories. But modern science would say that even a rock is nothing but a kind of wave. It is a specific configuration of energy vibrations existing as a modification of the wider field of energy. It does not exist by itself. Nor is its permanence everlasting. Time bites into it. Time gave it birth and will one day devour it. In ultimate analysis, change is the stuff of which it is made. For all its apparent solidity, it is indeed a wave of energy—a wave formed on the vast ocean of energy.

The same is true of the human individual. He is a highly evolved constellation of energy vibrations. He evolves to the extent that the novel and emergent quality of consciousness distinguishes him and sets him apart from the rest of creation. Compared with the rock, the human individual is a very feeble and broken reed. But he is a conscious reed. He overcomes his feebleness and fragility by being conscious of these characteristics. He even can overcome change and time by discovering his eternal relatedness to cosmic Being. Therein lies his glory. And his boundless possibility. Consciousness yields ever new insights into the structure of Being. It unfolds ever new values. So, the human being, conscious as he is, learns to determine his conduct by his unfolding vision of new values and determinants.

Man's freedom is a characteristic of his consciousness. There is no mysterious faculty within him which would be called free will. The notion of free will as a distinct faculty belongs to the exploded myth of old Faculty Psychology. Man is free to the extent of his increasing awareness of new possibilities, new ideas, new goals of life. As they are disclosed in his consciousness, he is being perpetually reborn. He is always breaking with the past, and beholding new visions of the future. His old determinants are discarded in favor of new ideas. Therein lies his freedom. Expanding consciousness is indeed of the essence of freedom. Freedom is not absence of all determination. It is the ability to renounce the determinism of instinct and blind impulse and to replace them by newly apprehended values and principles. By virtue of his unfolding consciousness, man is always breaking the bonds of the past and creatively advancing into the future. This spirit of creative advance is the reality of his freedom. And it is freedom which confers immortality upon him. The more he shakes loose from the fetters of ignorant attachment to the perishing things of time, the more he partakes of the immortality of the Eternal.

The Integral Theory of Immortality

We are now in a position to state briefly the integral theory of immortality. The integral view is the complete statement and logical culmination of the nondualistic approach of Vedānta.

Immortality is an attribute of enlightened consciousness. All men therefore have the potentiality of immortality by virtue of their consciousness. When the personality of an individual is harmonized and integrated, he attains enlightenment. He gains insight into his existential oneness with the all-encompassing Being. The veil of ignorance and separative consciousness is lifted from his eyes. Feelings of fear and insecurity, anxiety and personal unworthiness, are overcome. There is an enlargement of Being and joyful participation in the life of the Infinite. In one word, an individual experiences immortality here and now.

But the experience of participation in the life eternal of the Infinite does not mean self-annihilation in the Infinite. Immortality is an attribute of consciousness, of enlightened existence, not of non-existence. What is annihilated on the attainment of immortality is not the self, but the ignorant and separative consciousness of the alien-ated self. The veil of ignorance torn apart, the individual self can now enter into real and fruitful union with the eternal. When the finite space enclosed within a house becomes aware of its existential oneness with the infinite space, the house does not get demolished. When a par-ticular wave becomes aware of the fact that it is the ocean itself in an individualized mode, it does not perish as a wave. Similarly, when a human individual becomes aware of his inmost self as it is, namely, as an active center of the one undivided Being, it does not get lost and liqui-dated. On the contrary, it shines with all the glory of the Supreme Being.

The true meaning of immortality has often been ob-scured by the confusion between the goal of life and the end of life. The doctrine of liberation or *mokṣa* in Ve-dānta has two subtle implications. *Mokṣa* may mean the highest goal of life, namely, spiritual enlightenment. It may also mean the final end or terminus of an individual-ized form of existence, its re-absorption in the formless eternity. Confusion between these two meanings of *mokṣa* has often been responsible for much misguided spiritual endeavor.

Higher mysticism rightly affirms that all individualized forms of existence have an end in time. No individualized form has any need to endure for eternity, for instance, for billions of years. Nor is there any sense in that. The doctrine of personal immortality in the sense that a per-son must be rewarded for his virtue with continued exist-ence for billions of years without end is an illusion of the ignorant mind. It is the sublimated wish-fulfillment of the unconscious psyche. It represents the egotistic desire of the unenlightened. It springs from one's blind attach-ment to the individualized form of one's being. It is the result of ignorant identification with the body, gross or subtle, physical or psychic. So, Vedānta and Buddhism rightly affirm that the individual as a particular existent is bound one day to be reabsorbed into the Infinite, whether conceived as formless Being or as Nonbeing. That is the ultimate chronological end of all life. Not to be able to accept this ultimate end fearlessly and cheerfully is a mark of ignorance and egotism.

But the unfortunate thing is that many spiritual seekers and mystics look upon the ultimate end as also the goal of life. The goal of life is enlightenment, not annihilation in the formless Being. It is self-realization, not self-liquidation. It is the transformation of the ego, the I-sense, not its total destruction. It is the knowledge of things as they are, not the destruction of the self as it is. But, on account of the confusion in this respect, some mystics set before themselves the goal of self-annihilation in the Absolute. In consequence, they follow the policy of withdrawal from life and society. They tread the path of slow but sure suicide. They smother the will to live, and unconsciously yield to the dark death-wish slumbering in their psyche.

The most valid spiritual ideal of life is to transform one's whole being into an image of the Divine, and not to get lost in the abyss of the Infinite. When an individual learns to live as an individual, that is, as a unique creative center of the Eternal, he attains living immortality (*jīvanmukti*).

It may be said that authentic immortality has four essential aspects. First, immortality implies an individual discovery of the nontemporal dimension of his existence. To discover the nontemporal depth is to experience essential oneness with the Eternal, here and now, while living in the flesh. This may be described as living immortality (*jīvanmukti*). It is reflected in the statement "I am in essence one with the Supreme (*Brahman*)."

Secondly, immortality implies conscious union with the Infinite, without loss of personal existence or individuality. It is participation in the life of the Infinite without loss of freedom and personality. The I-sense is not liquidated, but purged of impurities. It bursts through the shell of separative consciousness and experiences itself as a unique and active center of the cosmic whole. Individuality is not lost, but illuminated. Emancipated from the fetters of egocentricity, it becomes cosmocentric. This may be called existential immortality (*sarvātma bhāva*).

Thirdly, immortality implies intelligent participation in the creative advance of life. Not egotistically with blind attachment and with consequent fear, anxiety, ambition and impatience. But in a spirit of nonattachment and with creative vision of the future, in harmony with the cosmic purpose of life. Immortality now assumes the form of conscious cooperation with the cosmic force of evolution—with the dynamic world-spirit. There is a sense of deathless continuity in such a spirit of cosmic cooperation. This may be called evolutionary immortality (*sādharmya mukti*).

Finally, the concept of immortality implies a harmonization of the entire personality and a transformation of the physical organism as an effective channel of expression of higher values. This may be called material immortality (*rūpāntar mukti*).

There are some mystics and spiritual seekers who strengthen and purify their bodies just enough to be able to experience the thrilling touch of the Divine. They use the body as a ladder, by climbing which the pure spiritual level—the domain of immortality—is to be reached. On attaining that level, the body is felt as a burden, as a prison house, as a string of chains that holds one in bondage. Disssociation from this last burden of the body is considered *a sine qua non* for complete liberation. Continued association with the body is believed to be the result of the last lingering trace of ignorance (*avidyā leśa*). When the residual trace of ignorance is gone, the spirit is finally set free from the shackles of the body.

The above view is based upon a subtle misconception about the purpose of life and the significance of the body. The body is not only a ladder that leads to the realm of immortality, but also an excellent instrument for expressing the glory of immortality in life and society. It is capable of being thoroughly penetrated by the light of the spirit. It is capable of being transformed into what has been called the "Diamond Body." As a result of such transformation, the body does not appear any more to be a burden upon the liberated self. On the contrary, it becomes a perfect image of the self. It shines as the Spirit made flesh. It functions as a very effective instrument for creative action and realization of higher values in the world. It is purged of all inner tension and conflict. It is liberated from the anxiety of repressed wishes. It is also liberated from the dangerous grip of the death impulse born of self-repression. Mystics who look upon the body as a burden suffer from the anxiety of self-repression and the allurement of the death wish.

Material immortality means decisive victory over both of these demons. It conquers the latent death instinct in man, and fortifies the will to live as long as necessary, as a channel of expression of the Divine. It also liquidates all forms of self-suppression and self-torture and self-mutilation. As a result the total being of an individual becomes strong and steady, whole and healthy. There is a free flow of psychic energy. It is increasingly channeled into ways of meaningful self-expression. Under the guidance of the indwelling light of the eternal, it produces increasing manifestation of the spirit in matter.

Chapter 15

THE PROBLEM OF EVIL

The problem of evil is one of the most baffling and persistent problems of our life. It stares us in the face, however much we may philosophize and try to argue it out of existence. We may fly on the wings of fancy into a world of all joy and radiance, but the moment we come down to our *terra firma*, the existence of evil assumes the frightful proportions of a final inexplicability. Reflection upon the nature of evil has indeed been the starting-point of most daring adventures of the human spirit. It is a riddle which life, like Sphinx, constantly poses to us. The deepest movements of life have always sprung from an attempt at its solution.

Statement of the Problem

David Hume's statement of the problem of evil is classical. The inescapable presence of evil in life seems to make the divine attributes of all-wise and all-good incompatible with the attribute of all-powerful. A God who is essentially good can hardly tolerate His creation being disfigured by endless sufferings and miseries, and by tragic frustrations and anomalies. If then God is an all-good Being, either He is not all-powerful, or He is not all-wise. Either His noble intentions are thwarted by some malicious forces of darkness, or He is out-witted by superior diabolical powers.

If omniscience be affirmed to be of the essence of God, then either His holiness is to be questioned, or He must be declared powerless as against the superior might of the devil.

If again one insists upon equating God with omnipotence, one must be prepared to see either wisdom, or goodness or both departing from the Divine Nature. It is inconceivable that the omnipotence of an all-wise and all-good God should not be employed to crush all hostile opposition with a view to making His creation a thing of perfect beauty and seamless harmony. If God be omnipotent, but neither omniscient nor holy, then God ceases to be God, and is lost into the darkness of some blind physical energy. That would be a solution of the problem of evil at the cost of our deep-rooted faith in the reality of the Divine. Instead of being a patient untying, it would be an impatient, one-stroke cutting asunder of the knot of evil. With blind matter as the source of all existence, and with mechanical law as the support of all becoming, the deepest aspirations of our life would be stultified, and the profoundest revelations of the Spirit set at naught.

Reflection upon the problem of evil has given rise to many interesting extremes of philosophic thinking. While some have tried to solve the problem by denying the reality of God, some have impugned the very existence of evil. While some have looked upon evil as a permanent feature of reality, some have reduced to unreality not only the phenomenon of evil but even the world itself. We shall pass in review some representative attitudes of thought in regard to the problem of evil, and then show that evil is neither a permanent, unconquerable feature of reality, nor a sphere of unreality or illusion. It is rather an incidental circumstance of the gradual process of self-manifestation of Reality. It is a real factor of life, which, for all its reality, is capable of being subdued.

Dualistic Submission to Evil

There are some philosophers who prefer to sacrifice the absoluteness of the Divine in order to make room for evil. They posit an alien principle or hostile power on which the responsibility for evil can be foisted.

Plato, for instance, postulates Nonbeing and holds that the world of our experience is compounded of Being and Nonbeing. Nonbeing is the basic, formless stuff out of which the universe has been fashioned. The tragic features of our life are to be traced to the fact that the patterns of perfection (ideas or forms) can receive only an imperfect, and often clumsy, embodiment in the medium of nonbeing, or formless matter. To put it in plain language, the good intentions of God are in a large measure thwarted by the recalcitrant stuff which matter or nonbeing is. Hence the evil that disfigures the creation of God.

While Plato traces the phenomenon of evil to formless matter or nonbeing, Zoroastrianism traces it to a kind of evil god. Zoroastrianism takes its stand upon the unmitigated dualism of two ultimate principles which are radically opposed to each other. One is a good God, Ahura Mazda, and the other is an evil God, Ahriman. The world is a battle-ground of these two hostile powers. All that is good and beautiful, lofty and noble, sublime and harmonious, is to be set down to the credit of Ahura Mazda. And whatever is ugly and abominable, tragic and repulsive, sinful and discordant in our life, is an indication of the active presence of Ahriman.

Some East African tribes solve the problem with utmost simplicity. Their solution is perfectly in tune with Zoroastrian dualism, only stated in a cruder form. They hold that all the good things of life come from God who is all good, but every now and then God's good intentions and noble plans are thwarted by his half-witted, half brother. This half brother is often quite intolerable, but goodness prevents the big brother from killing him.

Dualism in some form or other—dualism that drives a wedge between the imperfect world of actuality and the perfect world of values—appears in widely divergent schools of philosophic thinking. The Sāṁkhya school of Indian philosophy postulates the absolute dualism of matter and spirit, *Prakṛti* and *Puruṣa,* the dynamic source of all variations and the static poise of timeless perfection. The evils and imperfections of our life flow from lack of discrimination on the part of the individual as to these entirely divergent principles. They are a necessary consequence of the Spirit's self-identification with unconscious Nature through beginningless non-discrimination (*anādi aviveka*). Our body, life, mind, and intellect, are but different modifications of Nature so that it is a colossal mistake to regard them as integral factors in the life of the Spirit. All our sufferings and miseries are the penalties we have to pay for that initial mistake—for our original sin of eating from the tree of objective or empirical consciousness.

William James, the celebrated pragmatist, looks upon evil as the rock on which all forms of monism are wrecked. Perpetual conflict in our life between Light and Darkness opens before him a pluralistic universe, in which side by side with the forces of evil there is also "an ideal tendency in the nature of things." God is, in his view, not a unique all-comprehensive reality, not an omnipotent sovereign who rules over all that he surveys. God is just a superior power who is immensely greater than man and who is constantly tending towards the realization of higher values. His triumph over the forces of darkness is not a *fait accompli,* not a pre-destined certainty, but is conditional upon the right type of cooperation from man. The world is not a deterministic scheme, not a scene for "the rattling off of a chain forged innumerable years ago." It is a melioristic universe that we live in, a universe in which we have just a fighting chance of safety.

The above tendency to equate God with Goodness and at the same time to reduce Him to "an each among eaches," or to a "primus inter pares"—to a Being who has always to contend with powerful opponents—has found favor with many ethically minded philosophers. But a limited God, a God who is simply good but not infinite and absolute, can function neither as the Ultimate of philosophy nor as the highest category of religious interpretation. The reality of one all-comprehensive Being sustaining the bewildering variety of phenomenal existence is an immediate certainty of the profoundest spiritual experience. No amount of difficulty in the way of our reflective understanding, and no amount of protestation by the senses, can override that immediate certainty. So the hypothesis of a pluralistic or dualistic universe torn by perpetual conflict between irreducibly ultimate powers is inconsistent with the fundamental intuitions of mankind.

Pantheistic Denial of Evil

Those who have caught a glimpse of the Spirit in its ineffable purity are often inclined to overlook the obdurate presence of evil. Their eyes too full of the light of the Spirit, they fail to make a realistic approach to the dark and gloomy features of life. Pantheism is the product of such one-sided perception. It seeks to explain evil away, rather than attempt a sincere and systematic explanation thereof. The phenomenon of evil is, in the view of pantheism, a mere appearance, a passing illusion. It is entirely relative to our sensuous imagination, to our narrow and ignorant way of thinking. Evil is bound to melt away upon the emergence of a total and comprehensive view of reality, a view of reality *sub specie aeternitatis*. It takes all sorts to make a thing of beauty. To produce a picture of unimpeachable beauty, what is needed is a judicious combination of different shades of color, dark as well as bright—a skillful mixture of shade and light. The dark shades of the picture appear ugly only to an all-too-analytical seeing, which knows not how to appreciate beauty. To a synthetic appreciation—even the darkest spots reveal themselves as elements of a marvellous harmony. The picture is a thing of spotless beauty, not in spite of, but because of, all the spots that it is made to contain.

But how far can the above analogy carry us? Is the cosmic situation analogous to the harmony of an aesthetic product? It seems to us that the pantheistic denial of evil is based upon the fallacy of false analogy. A painting or picture is a frozen image of reality. It is an abstraction from the flux of existence. It can never represent reality in its concrete fullness. It is the artist's snapshot view or perspective of the real at a given moment. The static picture, for all its harmony and beauty, can, by no means, reproduce the dynamic flow of the real in its concrete mobility. Nor can it represent Being in its multidimensional fullness.

In contemplating a great work of art we admire its beauty and perfection. But at the same time we know that it is a finished product. It expresses the artist's emotional reaction to reality viewed from a certain angle.

In contemplating life in its livingness, we are vividly aware of the fact that it is an unfinished business. So, our reaction is twofold. On the one hand, we respond with joy and admiration. If we have any philosophic insight or spiritual wisdom, we are in a position to appreciate the beauty of life as a moving image of eternity. We see how the glory of the eternal is reflected in the multicolored richness of life. And when the ontological insight is integral, our comprehension of the meaning of life gains full depth. We have a feeling of re-awakening by the shocking challenge of life. Life appears to us not only as beauty, but also as duty. Life discloses to us not only its glory, but also its boundless potentialities. It is not enough to contemplate evil as a natural part of life and thus develop an attitude of peaceful resignation. An integral vision of truth is bound to inspire a creative urge. It is sure to induce a complex emotional reaction, such as combines wonder with creative inspiration, admiration with compassion, peace with action.

An integral insight into the structure of Being reveals life as the creative adventure of the eternal in time. It lights up the dynamic potentialities of existence. It opens up ever new possibilities waiting to emerge in the course of evolution. Consequently, evil appears not just as the shadow of good to be tolerated. It comes as a challenge to be boldly faced and overcome. It is the power of darkness which can be dispelled by the power of light. When thus overcome, it gives rise to new values. But if tolerated or connived at in a spirit of slothful resignation, the reign of darkness is further consolidated.

Pantheism is passive submission to evil as a product of ignorance. The argument is that since life on the whole is good as an image of God, evil as a necessary part of life must be an element of goodness, too. To think otherwise is ignorance. Evil is an illusion insofar as it is the result of ignorance. So, wisdom lies in accepting evil as a contributory factor in the divine beauty of Life. Such a line of thinking is crystallized in the dictum: Whatever is, is good. Whatever happens is the will of God. The invisible hand of God is there, behind all events. Does not God dwell equally in all men, saints and sinners alike? Is not God at the helm of all affairs, prosperity and adversity, freedom and bondage, war and peace?

This is very dangerous teaching indeed. Dangerous, not because it is false, but because it is a half-truth, mixed up with falsehood. Of course, God is present in all, saints and sinners alike. But that does not make the sin committed by a sinner good or the expression of the divine will. God is present in both saints and sinners as the fundamental spiritual potentiality of man as man. Sinful actions are a violation of that spiritual potentiality. They are a violation of the essential nature of man as a spark of the Divine. Sinful actions such as murder out of greed, wanton destruction for fun, treachery, robbery, kidnapping, raping, etc. are a profanation of one's latent divinity. In the life of a saint, the indwelling divinity is brought to some degree of manifestation. In the case of a sinner, it remains suppressed. Nonetheless, it is not totally absent. That is why the possibility of a sinner turning into a saint is always there. Condemnation of evil or sin is the human way of calling the sinner's attention to this potential divinity. But sinfulness must be regarded as a reprehensible fact of existence to be condemned and overcome.

The attitude of passive resignation to all the happenings of life has, to be sure, a spiritual quality. It is conducive to personal purity and peace of mind. It also generates some amount of transforming power. For instance, when a saint refuses to recognize the sinfulness of a sinner and embraces him with genuine love in his heart, he may work thereby a conversion of consciousness in the sinner. But this does not prove the unreality of the sinner's acts of sinfulness. It proves the superior reality and power of love and wisdom. Evil is not unreal, but an inferior reality. It is not to be tolerated but transmuted by the power of the spirit. When practised by those who have not the ability to conquer and transform evil, the motto of 'No Evil' would amount to cowardice and connivance. So, the great poet Tagore very rightly observed that a person who connives at evil is no less guilty than a person who perpetrates evil. Both of them deserve to burn in the wrath of divine justice.

When practiced on the social level, the pantheistic doctrine of no-evil proves all the more disastrous. It encourages an attitude of careless indifference and apathy to the ills and evils of society, such as illiteracy, poverty, child mortality, unsanitary living conditions, uncontrolled family enlargement, unbridled greed in trade and commerce, selfish complicity in tyrannical rule or foreign domination, etc. It lends support to the policy of withdrawal from society for the sake of personal purity and salvation. The spirit of reform and social reconstruction is laid in cold storage. There is an abdication of responsibility for the betterment of life under the shallow pretext of religious piety.

The metaphysical truth that evil is an offspring of ignorance does not make evil unreal. Ignorance itself is a positive evil to be conquered. Divine omnipresence, rightly understood, provides no justification for resignation to evil. On the contrary, it should inspire us with boundless self-confidence in fighting God's battle for the reign of peace and love. It should give us strength in fighting Kṛṣṇa's battle in establishing the kingdom of *dharma,* that is to say, truth, justice and righteousness in human society. Evil is a positive force of ignorance that offers resistance to higher evolution. It is a real obstruction to the vision of higher values. At its worst, it is the ugly face of human stupidity. It is a power of darkness that devours the values that we cherish. At its best, it is a stimulating challenge to life.

Theistic Interpretation of Evil as Perversity of Will

Theism rejects the view that ignorance (*avidyā*) is the root cause of evil. In its view, evil stems not from ignorance but from the perversity of will. The perversity of will is a symptom of the evil doer's subjection to Satan or the devil. Criminal action is the result of the devil's overpowering influence in the life of the criminal.

A man, for example, knows that robbing a bank or killing a person for money is an evil. But still he goes ahead and commits the crime in spite of his knowledge that it is a crime. He chooses evil out of greed and selfishness. Evidently his choice is determined, not by his ignorance, but by his perversity of will.

Let us analyze the situation a little closely. When a person robs a bank or kills a person, what is his mental condition? Probably, he is in the grip of an overmastering impulse to rob or kill. Considerations of good and evil are simply shut out of the mind. His entire being becomes one irresistible urge to commit the crime. The person himself may not know why he is doing it. But he cannot help doing it. Psychoanalysis rightly diagnoses it as 'mental sickness'. The notion of a mysterious will power causing such sickness or capable of preventing such sickness is just an unscientific myth. This myth is based upon the now exploded faculty psychology of medieval times. The mental sickness responsible for the irrational and compulsive criminal action is due to lack of insight into one's unconscious emotional conflicts. It is due to lack of insight into one's true identity, one's authentic self, one's purpose of life, and position in society. In one word, it is due to what is called *avidyā,* ontological ignorance, in the Hindu-Buddhist tradition.

Metaphysical ignorance (*avidyā*) does not mean ignorance about the laws of society. A criminal certainly violates a law of society in spite of his full knowledge about it. *Avidyā* is a much deeper kind of ignorance. It is ignorance about one's authentic self, and its ultimate relationship to the world. The removal of such basic ignorance is enlightenment, or authentic self-understanding. Criminality melts away like mist in the sunlight of adequate self-understanding.

We may also imagine that the criminal while performing a criminal action, such as robbing or shooting, may have some private reasons of his own justifying his deeds. In that case, he feels that his private reasons have priority over the rationality of social laws. He has here certain doubts about the wisdom of social laws. He may feel cheated by society. He may nurse strong resentment against society, on account of the hardship and suffering unjustly caused to him and his family by the existing social order. He may even believe that the existing social laws are basically unjust insofar as they are traceable to the greed and exploitation of the powers that be. He may think that they are a clever device of the privileged class to exploit the pure and illiterate masses. Or, he may believe that those who are responsible for the administration of social justice or enforcement of socioethical laws are themselves incorrigibly corrupt and hypocritical.

In the above-mentioned case, all that can be said is that the evil action of the criminal is due to his wrong judgment. He has a distorted view of his relationship to society, and of the moral basis of the social order. He has very imperfect knowledge about his ultimate self-interest and also about the effective means of righting a social wrong. Thus, we come back again to the conception of basic ignorance. It is ignorance about the self as related to society, or about the means and ends, which is the root cause of evil.

Theism considers original sin as the ultimate cause of human suffering. Now, what is this Original Sin? God commanded Adam and Eve, living in paradise, not to eat from the tree of knowledge. But, at the wily suggestion of the serpent they disobeyed the divine command. But, why did they disobey? Because they felt persuaded by the serpent that God did not want them to be all-knowing like God Himself. Knowledge would liberate them from childish dependence upon the divine authority. It would confer upon them a status of equality with God. This coincided splendidly with the secret desire of Adam and Eve. They wanted to outgrow their bondage to the apron strings of benevolent paternalism, however celestial. They wanted to have a life of their own and assert their own individuality and freedom. There is a joy of freedom in the very act of defying authority. Can we blame the earliest progenitors of the human race for this very noble desire to exercise their freedom, to attain independent growth, and acquire fuller knowledge for themselves?

If there was anything wrong about their defiance of the divine commandment, it was their ignorance. Ignorance about the precise nature of their ultimate self-interest; ignorance about the true motive of God; ignorance as to how to go about fulfilling their legitimate desires for fuller knowledge. So under closer scrutiny, original sin resolves itself into primal ignorance (*avidyā*). In flouting the divine will, Adam and Eve certainly knew that they were committing the wrong of disobedience. But they thought—whether rightly or wrongly—that it was through such disobedience that they could fulfil their desire for knowledge, power, freedom, and independent growth. Disobedience appeared to their mind a much lesser evil than subjugation to crippling authority and paternal despotism.

The serpent itself symbolizes this primal ignorance. It is the unconscious psychê. The whisper of the serpent that is heard denotes the suggestion and motivation that comes from the unconscious psyche. There is ignorance there. But there is also intuitive wisdom there. Imbedded in the unconscious are very meaningful impulses and drives for knowledge, for freedom, for power and self-existence. In order to achieve balanced growth of personality, one must come to terms with them. One must integrate them into the concrete texture of the evolving mind. One must patiently and tactfully channel them into the higher ends of existence.

Thus we see that evil in the form of human sinfulness is in ultimate analysis due not to any inexplicable perversity of a mysterious faculty of the mind such as free will. Nor is it due to the overpowering influence in man's life of any devil or Satan that exists independently of God. The root cause of sinfulness is nescience. Original sin is no other than basic ignorance about the authentic self (*ātman*) and its relatedness to Being (*Brahman*). The devil is no other than the positive power of such ignorance. Sri Aurobindo has shown in great detail and with utmost clarity how ignorance in various forms causes sin and suffering in human life.[1]

---

[1] Sri Aurobindo, *The Life Divine*, Vol. II, Part I, Ch. XI.

Chapter 16

EVIL, SUFFERING, AND GROWTH

It has been suggested by some that the reason for the existence of evil in the world is that it is through constant struggle with the forces of evil that personality can be developed and character molded. "Soul-making," they contend, is the typical business of the universe. In order to accomplish that end it is necessary that our life in the world should be a "chapter of accidents." The world is intended to be a "vale of soul-making," not a land of lotus-eating. It is in the medium of an apparently hostile environment that the moral fibre of character is strengthened and the heroic types of soul produced. If it appears to us that "contingency is writ large across the face of Nature," or that "there is an unfathomable injustice in the nature of things," we need not be overwhelmed by such appearances. It is the very contingent and tragic features of Nature which make her the fittest medium of development and excellent training ground of the soul.

It must be conceded that there is a profound truth in this view of the matter. We should not ignore the depth of insight that inspires it. But still the view of evil as an educative agency sounds, in the last analysis, like a sort of consolation philosophy. Lotze's criticism that a better and more decent machinery might have been devised by the Almighty for the molding of perfect souls is not without application to the above view. Even though all anguish and injustice, cruelties and tragedies might be forgotten in the attainment of holiness or an exalted state of beatitude, that does not justify as inevitable their having been suffered.[1]

It has been suggested that the cruelty and hostility of the world process is a means to the moral end of perfection so that the Absolute may thereby obtain an increasing enrichment of being. The contingency of the world is contributory to the perfection of the whole.[2] But can there be a further enrichment of That which is essentially perfect? Can there be any further addition to the perfection of the Absolute? Moreover, can the really perfect Being desire or permit an enrichment of being through terrible sufferings endured by others? Could not His own enrichment and the development of individual selves have been achieved through a system of means consistent with His loving and merciful nature?

The difficulty as to the fulfillment of the divine purpose through sufferings endured by others is further accentuated by the hypothesis of an extra-cosmic God. If God be of such a nature that He works out His own purpose through the intense sorrows and sufferings of other people, then we cannot help thinking of Him as an essentially undivine and satanic principle.

But, why start with the assumption that the Absolute is an extra-cosmic Deity? Or that God remains aloof from our sufferings, and that the cries of the human heart do but occasionally and faintly reach His ears? He is in truth indivisibly present in every man, and all creatures are but God Himself manifested in various forms. It is therefore God Himself who undergoes untold sufferings in the shape of human beings. And He does so for His own fuller manifestation in and through different individual centers. Suffering then is not to be conceived as God's device for the shaping of separate moral personalities. It is in fact an incidental circumstance accompanying the process of God's increasing self-manifestation in the apparent contraries of His nature.

---

[1] Herman Lotze, *Outlines of a Philosophy of Religion* (London: George Allen and Company, 1911), p. 144.

[2] A. Seth Pringle-Pattison, *The Idea of God,* p. 416.

Evil as Incidental Accompaniment of Spirit's Self-Manifestation in Matter

When Pringle-Pattison says that soul-making is the typical business of the universe, he utters indeed a profound truth. But this soul-making, the shaping and molding of unique personalities, is not surely intended to enrich the being of God. There can be no addition to perfection, no further enrichment of that infinitely rich Being who remains infinite even after an infinite is substracted from Him.

So the truth behind the molding of human personalities is the progressive manifestation of the Infinite in the finite, the increasing self-revelation of the Divine in human form, the gradual self-unfoldment of the Spirit in self-created conditions apparently opposed to, and *toto caelo* different from, His nature. The supreme is pure existence, pure knowledge, pure bliss. It seeks self-manifestation in such apparent contraries of its nature as the nonbeing, inconscience, and inertia of matter. This gives us the profoundest secret of the world-process, the deepest mystery of the cosmic drama. It is, as it were, the play of hide and seek between Spirit and Matter, between God and Nature. The Spirit first hides itself behind Nature, and then seeks its rediscovery through her evolutionary endeavors. Nature first gets separated from Spirit, and then seeks reunion through the finite's longing for the Infinite.

But is not God absolute bliss itself? If delight is the very stuff and essence of Divine Being, what point is there in asserting that God seeks delight through a protracted process of self-manifestation in apparent contraries of His nature? Fullness or abundance of delight can hardly be said to leave scope for any further longing after delight. Perfection renders meaningless all further seeking and yearning.

But on deeper reflection it will be found that the above criticism rests upon a poor idea about the divine delight.

Why limit the essence of Being to one form of delight only, to the delight of immutable being, or to the unvarying delight of timeless self-absorption? There is, as Sri Aurobindo points out,[3] a delight of becoming as much as a delight of being, a delight of change and movement as much as a delight of permanent tranquility. The essence of the delight of becoming consists in unending creation, or to put it more philosophically, in expressing in infinite time the infinite possibilities that are inherent in the infinite. In its intrinsic being, the supreme Spirit is above all change and movement, and is surely self-sufficient in its pure delight. But the Spirit has also an aspect of becoming, an aspect of free creation and self-expression. Its delight of becoming consists in the variable manifestation of the infinite possibilities of its being. It is the self-expansive urge of the delight of becoming which accounts for its will to manifest in the contraries of its nature. The self-luminous Spirit makes a plunge into the dark inconscience of matter in order that through a conquest of darkness the glories of spirit may be manifested in material conditions. Evil is the name we give to the obstruction and hostility of the material medium to the creative self-expression of the Spirit.

Lotze is perfectly right when he says that evil is due not to the uniform operation of a system of natural laws, but to the inner nature and changeability of the "things merely given which might be otherwise, and whose reality depends on the Divine activity."[4] Following the guidance of reason, he sees no way of reconciling the fact of evil with our conception of the Divine. So he abandons in despair all rational approach to the problem and chooses to fall back upon God's inscrutable wisdom.

Plato maintains that the ultimate source of all evil is nonbeing or intractable matter. In order to vindicate the absolute purity of God and the incorruptibility of the Form of the Good, he interposes a yawning chasm of onto-

[3] *The Life Divine*, p. 123.

[4] Hermann Lotze, *Outlines of a Philosophy of Religion* (London: George Allen & Company Ltd., 1911), pp. 142-43.

logical discontinuity between nonbeing and being, matter and form, nature and soul. This is obviously a kind of unmitigated dualism. Whereas Lotze in stressing the fundamental unity and ultimate goodness of existence takes shelter behind divine inscrutability, Plato gives up the attempt at any final reconciliation. He is frankly satisfied with a dualistic position—the dualism of matter and form, existence and essence.

But cannot a final reconciliation be achieved, without either invoking the inscrutable as Lotze does, or resorting to dualism as Plato does? What if matter or nonbeing, which causes by its recalcitrance the tragic features of life, be, in ultimate analysis, a form of expression of the Spirit itself? It is quite possible, as mystics suggest, that matter is the objective manifestation of the spirit under the aspect of space-time. It is no other than spirit in a state of involution in its apparent opposite, to wit, inconscience, so that inconscient Nature by her evolutionary endeavor may progressively realize the riches of spirit in the realm of externality. Matter is indeed, in ultimate analysis, the lowest limit of self-alienation of the self-luminous spirit. For all its apparent inertia, hostility and recalcitrance, it provides an excellent stage on which the exciting drama of life is enacted.

Pain as Abnormal to Our Being

The problem of suffering is particularly acute for those who look upon the world as a manifestation of the fullness of divine delight. Granted that matter is the source of all sufferings that torment our embodied existence. Granted further that "eternal and immutable delight of being moving out into infinite and variable delight of becoming" is the root-cause of the Spirit's falling asleep in matter with a view to re-awakening in unique conditions. But still the question would arise: is not the essential painfulness of embodied existence an outrage upon the nature of the Spirit which is made of the stuff of pure delight? Is not there a palpable incongruity between the inherent delight of the Spirit and the endless suffering of its manifestation?

It should be pointed out here that the view that our life is essentially and overwhelmingly painful is an error of our perspective. It is an exaggeration due to the magnifying power of our emotional susceptibiltiy. To a detached and dispassionate view of the matter the sum of pleasure is sure to appear far greater than the sum of pain, suggestions to the contrary notwithstanding. The universal and overpowering instinct of self-preservation and the overmastering will-to-live present in all creatures, are to be traced to the immanence of delight in existence. Pain affects us much more intensely, and the sum of pain looms much larger than the greater sum of pleasure, precisely because pain is abnormal to our being, contrary to our natural tendency, and is experienced as an outrage on our existence, an offence and a shocking blow to what we are and what we seek to be. The normal satisfaction of our existence which is always there regardless of objective circumstances affects us as something neutral and as neither palpably pleasant nor painful. It is because pleasure is normal that we do not treasure it, hardly even observe it, unless it intensifies into some acuter form of itself, into a wave of happiness, a crest of joy or ecstasy.

Pain as a Consequence of Pent-up Evolutionary Energy

Researches in modern anthropology lend support to the view that pain is an indication of the undue hoarding or storing of that primal creative energy which is intended for further evolution. "All pain is a measure, if a crude one," says Gerald Heard, "of the degree of vital creative energy in any creature, animal or man." The animal does not suffer much because he is a living fossil; there is not much of unused vital energy within him. The savage suffers most when injured, because there is a huge reservoir of untapped evolutionary energy within him which is wasted in suffering. A cultured man, a man given to the higher pursuits of life, or, in other words, engrossed in creative endeavors, does not suffer much, because he succeeds in drawing off an amount of his pent-up energy and in directing it along higher channels.

The acute sufferings of the present day are due to the fact that our evolution, balked and thwarted, lopsided and unbalanced, has reached an unprecedented crisis. Prevented from a gradual expansion or a growing universalisation, our consciousness has been strangulated into separative egoism, both individual and collective. Since then suffering is a pathological symptom of evolution balked and thwarted, there must be a way out of it, and that way lies in letting the evolutionary energy resume in us the work of universal harmony through a radical change of our consciousness.

It is entirely wrong to suppose that suffering is an inherent and inalienable feature of life. What is needed to get out of suffering is not to turn one's back upon Life and its divergent currents. The root-cause of suffering is not the will-to-live, but rather a failure to cooperate with the growing evolution of the creative energy. The remedy for suffering is to release the pent-up primal energy to allow it to energize higher centers of consciousness and to lift ourselves out of the stagnant pools of strangulated individualized consciousness. As Henri Bergson maintains, it is through dynamic self-identification with the creative impetus—the impetus which is all-embracing love—that we can aspire to a state of unalloyed joy which is beyond all mixed feelings of pleasure and pain.

Suffering as a Non-Essential Passing Feature of Life

That suffering is not an essential or inalienable feature of life but only a passing phase, a vanishing quantity, has been demonstrated by Sri Aurobindo in his *The Life Di-*

vine. Suffering is the shadow cast by evolving ignorance in its gradual movement towards knowledge. Or, to look at it from another side, pain and pleasure are alike distorted reflections on the surface, or on the screen of ignorance which envelops our surface being, of the secret delight of existence. They serve a transitional end, and appear on close examination to be an outcome and arrangement of our imperfect evolution.

Pleasure, pain and neutral feeling are, so observes Sri Aurobindo, mechanical reactions of our nervous and mental being to the touches or shocks of the external world. There is no absoluteness or necessity in these reactions except the necessity of habit. The habit, however, ought to change in the course of evolution. It can be changed by a strong will to evolve. It is common knowledge that things which are agreeable to some are disagreeable to others, and appear either agreeable or disagreeable to the same individual in different conditions or at different stages of development. Our mind is more flexible in its responses to the world's touches than the nervous being which is more a slave of habit and more accustomed to a certain constancy of response. To our nervous being, victory, success, honor and good fortune of all kinds are pleasant things in themselves, absolutely; whereas their opposites such as defeat, failure, disgrace, and bad fortune of all kinds, appear to be unpleasant things in themselves, absolutely. But experience shows that man can rise above this necessity of habitual reactions, and can meet all the shocks of the world either with a perfect indifference or with an equal gladness.

But what is the reason behind these habits of response which account for the triple vibration of pleasure, pain and indifference of our sensational being? It seems to us that these habits of reaction are the devices of Nature for the protection of imperfectly developed beings against the attack of external forces. From the standpoint of the individual, the world is a play and a complex of multitudinous forces. Some of these forces are unfavorable to the individual at his present stage of imperfect growth, and so he recoils or shrinks from them through pain. The Sanskrit term *jugupsā* is very appropriate to denote this attitude of recoil or shrinking. The shocks and touches which are favorable appear pleasant and thrilling. This diversity of reaction continues so long as the soul is subject to matter and to egoistic limitation of the mind. At the present stage of development, the consciousness-force within us is extremely limited, cut off as it is by primal ignorance from the universal consciousness-force. So it cannot receive equally and calmly the multifarious shocks of the world. Pain and pleasure, as Sri Aurobindo puts it,[5] are in truth but currents, one imperfect and the other perverse but still currents—positive and negative currents, —of the same delight of existence. Owing to the egoistic limitation of our being and the strangulation of our consciousness, we cannot properly receive these currents and perceive the *rasa,* the essence of delight, which is in everything. Art and poetry give us a glimpse into this universal *rasa* through a detached and delightful representation of the sorrowful, the terrible, and even the horrible or repellent.[6] The aesthetic perception of currents is however only a partial and imperfect representation of the delight of existence, and it is conditioned by the liberation of one part of our nature from practical attachment or egoistic craving.

The pure delight in all things, the *rasa* in the heart of all existence, is in truth supra-mental and supra-aesthetic in character. An adequate experience of this delight is possible only through our liberation in all the parts of our nature. It is the "universal aesthesis, the universal standpoint of knowledge, the universal detachment from all things and yet sympathy with all in our nervous and emotional being,"[7] which alone can give us an access to the universal *rasa* in its purity. While the aesthetic atti-

---

[5] *The Life Divine,* p. 117.

[6] Ibid., p. 129.

[7] Ibid., p. 130.

tude is one of passive contemplation of the underlying harmony and beauty, the spiritual attitude is one of active participation in the creative delight. The aesthetic attitude considers sorrow, terror, horror and disgust as features of existence in spite of which an underlying harmony is percevied to be there. The spiritual attitude, instead of stopping short at a mere perception of the underlying harmony, proceeds actively to eliminate all discrepant and painful features of life in response to a deeper realization and with a view to a fuller manifestation of the pure unalloyed joy which is hidden in the heart of things.

Different Modes of Reaction to Suffering

Four different stages may be distinguished in one's attitude to sorrow and suffering. An individual's instinctive reaction to pain is, as has already been observed, one of immediate recoil and shrinking (*jugupsā*). Such a reaction has a purpose to fulfil so long as the soul remains bound to the fetters of ego-centric existence. An aspiration to grow into the freedom of a fuller life in harmony with others must replace *jugupsā* by *titikṣā,* that is to say, must replace the attitude of shrinking and contraction by that of boldly facing, enduring and conquering all shocks of existence. The spirit of brave endurance and conquest further leads on to what has been called Equality (*Samatā*).

This equality or equanimity of mind may be of two kinds. First, there is what may be called equal indifference to all external contacts. This consists in the maintenance of unperturbable calm and balance of mind in the presence of the dualities of existence. The stoic indifference to pains and pleasures, to joys and sorrows alike, and the ascetic detachment and serenity in the face of life's vicissitudes, are expressions of this sort of equality. This equal indifference or passive non-responsive serenity is based upon perception of the transcendental element in our nature.

There is, however, also a deeper kind of equality or poise of being such as springs from an integral realization of the Spirit both in its cosmic universality and supra-cosmic transcendence. Such equality does not express itself as an equal indifference to all contacts, but as an equal gladness in all contacts. It may be described as spiritual equality, to which all the world's touches are but messages of joy. It is born of freedom from egoity and a consequent perception of everything in its inmost essentiality. Sustained by the delight of being, it proceeds to participate in the variable delight of becoming. As a result, it actively issues in an unceasing effort towards a fuller manifestation of that creative delight. The equal reception of all events as variations of delight is not necessarily always the result of an indirect process running through different stages. It can also be straightway developed, as Sri Aurobindo points out, through a direct transformation[8] of the triple vibration of pain, pleasure and indifference into *ānanda* or pure delight, although such a direct transformation is exceedingly difficult for an average person.

Ethical Aspect of the Problem of Suffering

The ethical aspect of the problem of suffering calls for some consideration before the chapter can be brought to a close. Why is it that God invents torture as a means of test or as a passport to a fuller mode of life? Is not such a God inferior to the highest moral ideal that animates His creatures? Is suffering to be regarded as a mode of punishment that God inflicts for the sins committed by men? But sins are in fact born of man's limited knowledge and his limited powers, his ignorance and his weakness, which are ultimately traceable to the creative act of God himself. The real cause of sin is not indeed the freedom of man, but rather his inadequate freedom, his subjection to the cravings and desires of the lower nature. Responsi-

---

[8] Ibid., p. 130.

bility for the human soul's entanglement in the lower nature, or nondiscriminating self-identification therewith, must ultimately be borne by God himself.

But all these difficulties can be set down to one initially wrong supposition, namely that God is an extracosmic Being, an external ethical Personality, who conducts the business of creating and governing all creatures according to some eternally fixed ethical principles. This is a subtle form of anthropomorphism—an application of the characteristics of human nature to the understanding of the significance of the world-process. The view of the world as the handiwork of an extracosmic Deity belongs to the primitive phase of philosophic thinking. It has been our contention that the world is a spontaneous outpouring of creative joy in the heart of the Supreme. And the Supreme is dynamically present in the world. It is the Supreme itself in human form that undergoes the varied experiences of pleasure and pain with a view to a richly diversified manifestation of the joy of self-expression. The sinfulness and inherent self-discrepancy of man marks a stage in the movement of the Spirit from the inconscience of material Nature towards the superconscient harmony of gnostic existence, from an existence of blind uniformity and iron necessity to a life of luminous unity and complete freedom, perfect mutuality and profoundest love.

Western thinkers like F. H. Bradley and Bernard Bosanquet had the depth of insight to realize that the ethical point of view could by no means be treated as absolute. The moral distinctions are relative to a definite transitional stage in the self-unfoldment of the Absolute. As such they must not be used as a key to the interpretation of ultimate reality. Relative as they are to the divided consciousness of man, they are bound to change, and change radically, when he grows into the undivided consciousness of the Absolute. At the prehuman levels are nonmoral or infra-ethical modes of existence. The inherent self-discrepancies of human morality point to its self-completion in a supramoral consciousness such as would lay the foundation of a far better and fuller life, the life of truth and beauty and freedom and love. The fundamental thing—that which is common to all grades of evolution—is the gradual unfolding and self-expression of the Absolute. At the human stage, whatever hurts this self-expression, whatever impedes the progressive development of man's limited personality, is considered evil. On the contrary, whatever helps, stimulates, ennobles it, is accounted good. With the gradual development of the human personality, with the increasing self-expression of the Absolute within him, he must outgrow the morality of his divided consciousness and act spontaneously on the basis of a conscious realization of the absolute unity of all existence in the identity of the Absolute.

Conclusion

It is thus the evolutionary perspective which contains the best solution to the problem of evil. It throws a new light not only on moral evil but also upon physical evil. None of these different types of evil should be regarded as an inseparable aspect of life or a permanent feature of the world. As there can be no pain in the realm of inconscient matter, physical evil in the shape of pain and suffering enters the world with the emergence of life in the course of evolution. It is occasioned by the living being's incapacity for adequate reception of the contacts of the external world.

Moral evil enters the world with the emergence of the finite rational will in the course of evolution. It is occasioned not so much by an exercise of freedom as by man's inadequate freedom and subjection to the forces of darkness and ignorance. True freedom belongs not to the mental will, but to the Self. It is possible that at the next higher stage of evolution man will attain spiritual maturity by being lifted into the full freedom of the Self. That will mean the elimination of moral evil and the transformation of life into an expression of divine freedom and spontaneity.

It is also quite possible that at the suprahuman stage of evolution, inadequate reception of the world's external contacts will be replaced by a clear perception of the divine delight in all things and events. Blind attachment to exclusive particularity will be replaced by an expansion of consciousness to the dimensions of the entire universe. That will mean the elimination of sorrow and suffering and the transformation of life into a sacred poem of divine delight.

Integral self-development consists in overcoming man's primal ignorance in all its forms. It implies a growing spiritual insight into the essential structure of the Self and the supreme purpose of life. It also implies an intelligent and constructive channelling of unconscious drives and urges toward the creative fulfillment of one's authentic self. With the increasing elimination of primal ignorance from life and society, evil can be more and more conquered. Conquest of evil is an essential prerequisite to the kingdom of heaven on earth. The kingdom of heaven on earth is an heuristic maxim for actualizing man's profoundest potential here and now in this very world. It is the outflowering of the Divine in human society. It is the eventual triumph of light and love over darkness and hatred, of knowledge and freedom over ignorance and bondage, of justice and peace over barbarism and war.

Chapter 17

THE SUPERMIND AS INTEGRAL
CONSCIOUSNESS

Pivotal to the integral philosophy of Sri Aurobindo is the concept of the supermind. It provides the basis for his contention that such apparent opposites as matter and mind, nature, and spirit, world and God, the many and the One, are two inseparable poles of the same indivisible and all-comprehensive reality. It also enables him to affirm that normal sense perception on the one hand and the most exalted supersensuous mystic experience on the other are two termini of the same wide spectrum of multicolored human experience. And finally it shows him the way to the full integration of the social, economic, political, scientific, and technological values of life on the one hand and the esthetic, psychological, ethico-religious, and ontological values of existence on the other.

A brief analysis and evaluation of the manifold implications of the supermind will be provided in this chapter.

Total Awareness of Being

The supermind is integral consciousness. It is the awareness of Being in its integral fullness as distinguished from the mind's sectional or fragmentary cognition. The mind perceives the world piecemeal, section by section, item by item. It sees mountains, rivers, forests, and oceans —earth, moon, sun, and the stars—all existing separately from one another. It perceives the present moment in isolation from the past and the future. It perceives time in separation from space, and space-time in separation from the observing mind. But the supermind comprehends all the seemingly isolated data of perception as inseparably interrelated parts of the same cosmic whole.

That is why the comprehensive world-view as inspired by the integral consciousness of Being is called integral philosophy. And the art óf harmonious living in accord with the supramental vision of integral Being is known as integral or supermental yoga.

Whereas the mind is dualistic or dichotomous in its thinking, the supermind is nondual and nondichotomous in its comprehension. In trying to grasp the nature of the universe, the mind creates such dichotomies as mind and matter, nature and spirit, and the like. As a consequence, the continuity of the universe is broken. Intuitively aware of this fact, the mind then proceeds logically or dialectically to reconstruct that unity with the aid of all manner of intellectual schemes or conceptual structures, known as metaphysical systems. But an intellectual scheme of unity is at best a very poor substitute for the undivided and indivisible wholeness of Being.

There are three reasons why the mind in the mode of conceptual understanding fails to fathom the indivisible mystery of Being. First, it is governed by the formal laws of Aristotelian logic. If nature is nature, and spirit is spirit, how can the twain meet? If world is world, and God is God, how can the gulf be bridged? Secondly, since the intellect itself is a finite product of the free creativity of Being, no wonder that it fails to rise above its own limitations, just as a man can hardly jump over his own shoulders. Thirdly, the subject-object dichotomy being ingrained in the intellect, it knows not how to transcend that dichotomy except by undergoing a radical transformation.

The supermind is nondichotomous, because it intuitively grasps the ultimate unifying principle of creative freedom (*Mahāśakti*) which is one with Being. It is the self-light of Being itself dynamically present in man. So when man intuitively grasps the integral unity and fullness of Being, it is the power of Being itself brought to self-consciousness in man.

The Supermind and Synoptic Vision

Is the integral consciousness of the supermind the same as what Plato calls "synoptic vision"? There is indeed a striking similarity here, but also an important difference. Plato comprehends the universe as a whole in terms of eternal Ideas. The Idea of the Good which is the Idea of all Ideas is, for him, the ultimate unifying principle. But his logical idealism creates a new dichotomy—the dichotomy of facts and ideas, particulars and universals, existents and essences. Platonic philosophy furnishes no key to resolve this new dichotomy.

Hegel rolls all Platonic Ideas into one Absolute Idea by following the dialectical movement of categories. But since existence can hardly be derived from category, or idea or essence, whether conceived logically like Plato, or dialectically like Hegel, the dichotomy of actuality and ideality, existence and essence, facticity and category, remains unresolved.

The supermind penetrates to the heart of Being and discovers the ultimate unifying principle of the universe in the free creativity of Being. It is out of the fullness of Being's creative freedom that both the actual and the ideal, particulars and universals, existents and essences, facts and values, emerge into being. Springing from the same dynamic source, they intermingle as inseparable facets of the same creative flux.

Is supramental knowledge the same as Spinoza's vision of knowing things *sub specie aeternitatis?* Here again there is a striking similarity but not the relation of identity. Spinoza's ultimate principle is one infinite substance endowed with the parallel attributes of extension and thought. But substance-attribute is essentially a category of the human understanding. According to Immanuel

Kant it is inherent in the *a priori* structure of the understanding. In the view of Bertrand Russell, it is derived
from the structure of sentences composed of a subject and
a predicate. "It is a transference to metaphysics of what
is only a linguistic convenience."[1] Whether an *a priori*
form of perception or a structural form of language, the
notion of substance-attribute is a human mode of apprehension. In other words, it is a logical or linguistic con-
struct. So for Spinoza, God as the infinite substance is
the logical ground of the universe just as the definition
of a triangle is the logical ground of all its properties.
The properties of a triangle are eternally inherent in its
definition, but are essentially different from actual events
or happenings in time. And the definition of a triangle
has no potency to precipitate actual events in time. So
also Spinoza's infinite substance has no potency to produce actual occurrences in the realm of existence.[2]

Spinoza's infinite substance can aptly be described as
the lion's den to which all steps lead, but from which no
steps return. It cannot account for change, movement,
growth, evolution, generation of actual events, emergence
of fresh novelties, performance of free actions. So Spinoza's
knowledge *sub specie aeternitatis* provides us with a static
picture of the universe in which manifoldness is an eternally determined structure logically inherent in the One.

Supramental knowledge on the other hand is insight into the free boundless creativity of that nondual Being
which is the indivisible unity of existence and essence.
Change and evolution, growth and transformation, are
the stuff of which existing things of the world of manifestation are made. Whereas existence implies a definite position in the space-time continuum, essences imply comprehensive features of empirical existents as apprehended
by the human mind.

Sri Aurobindo distinguishes the supermind not only
from the mind but also from what he calls the overmind.

---

[1] Bertrand Russell, *A History of Western Philosophy* (New York:
Simon & Schuster, 1945), p. 201.

[2] Frank Thilly, *A History of Philosophy* (New York: Holt, 1936), p. 299.

Whereas the mind is sectional or fragmentary consciousness, and the supermind is integral consciousness, the
overmind is total or global consciousness.[3] For instance,
the overmind can grasp the material world as a whole, and
appreciate the predominant role and function of matter
as the basis and stuff of the material world, with such
other values as life, mind, and spirit gradually evolving
therein. But due to its lack of enduring experience and
operative knowledge of the ultimate unifying principle
of the universe, namely Being-Energy, it cannot eliminate
the discords and divisions, the conflicts and contradictions
of the material world. The supermind as the creative and
transforming knowledge of unity-in-diversity can alone
eliminate them and transform matter into a flawless and
transparent medium of manifestation of the glories of
Being.

The Supermind and Transcendent Wisdom

Is supramental knowledge the same as the transcendent
wisdom of the Buddha and Śaṁkara?

The wisdom of the Buddha consists in the realization
of the absolute Void or Nonbeing or Emptiness (*Śūnyatā*)
as the ultimate ground of the universe. The wisdom of
Śaṁkara consists in the realization of the absolutely indeterminate, attributeless Being (*Nirguṇa Brahman*) as
the ultimate ground. In final analysis, both indeterminate
Being and nameless Nonbeing mean the same thing.
There is no determination distinguishing the one from
the other. So the conclusion is irresistibly borne in upon
us that the world of space, time, manifoldness, and evolution is more or less unreal. It is an unreal superimposition
upon the indeterminate Being due to the operation of
Ignorance (*Avidyā*), according to Śaṁkara. It is an
evanescent, ephemeral phenomenon mysteriously appear-
ing in the absolute Void, according to the Buddha. It is
endowed only with some kind of conventional, pragmatic

---

[3] Sri Aurobindo, *The Life Divine* (New York: The Sri Aurobindo Library, 1951), pp. 257-262.

reality (*saṁvṛti satya*,[4] *vyavahārik sattā*[5]), according to both. Hence asceticism or monasticism inspired by total renunciation of the world is the highest spiritual ideal of life, in the view of both.

Integral philosophy advocates a complete shift in outlook. Being is not only the *ultimate* ground of the universe. It is also the dynamic, *creative* ground of the universe. It is "that from which all creatures are born, in which all abide, and into which all are dissolved again."[6] So it is the all-originating, all-sustaining, and all-dissolving power base of the universe. It is indeed indefinable and indeterminable inasmuch as it is beyond all anthropomorphic images and forms, beyond all abstract categories and concepts of the human mind. But it is erroneous to suppose that Energy or Creativity is a mere concept or category of thought.

Buddha made the mistake of assuming that Being is a mere category or subjective mode of interpretation of the human mind. And so he laid stress upon Nonbeing, Void, or Emptiness (*Śūnyatā*) as the ultimate philosophical principle, as the ground of all that is.

Now, what does Nonbeing, Void, or Emptiness precisely mean? Does it mean a metaphysical zero, the absolute negation of all being? In that case it cannot function as the ultimate ground and source of the variegated universe.

Nonbeing, construed as the absolute negation of all being, is an obvious contradiction in terms. Every negation presupposes a positive basis of affirmation. When we say: "There is nothing in this room; it is empty," we express our disappointment at not seeing any furniture or person in the room. But this disappointed declaration of "nothing" presupposes our perception of the room with an enclosed volume of space or space-time full of smoke and smell, oxygen and carbon dioxide, ants and rats, etc.

[4] D. T. Suzuki, *Outlines of Mahayana Buddhism* (New York: Schocken, 1963), p. 95. Also Nagarjuna, Madhuamika Shastra, Buddhist Text Society edition, pp. 180, 181.

[5] *The Brahma Sutra*, S. Radhakrishnan, trans. (New York: Harper, 1960), pp. 31, 33.

[6] *Taittiriya Upanishad,* III, I, I.

Does Nonbeing mean the absolute negation of all concepts? That also is self-contradictory. As soon as we use the word Nonbeing, we are expressing a concept. Since the concept has a mode of being of its own, we are dealing here also with a particular type of being. So absolute Nonbeing is again revealed as a flagrant contradiction in terms. Human language and thought cannot get along without concepts, symbols and words, just as the human body cannot jump over its own shoulders.

Does the concept of Nonbeing imply the conceptual or symbolical finger-pointing to the ultimate reality beyond all concepts and categories? That's better. Surely herein lies the true meaning of Buddha's Nonbeing. It is the finger-pointing to the ultimate reality beyond all logical notions and metaphysical categories. The name for that ultimate reality is nonconceptual, nondual being (*Nirguṇa Brahman*). So we find that Nonbeing is the linguistic device for the affirmation of the trans-conceptual fullness of Being.

Being as the transconceptual reality is the ultimate philosophical principle according to Śaṁkara. Buddha's Nonbeing, properly understood, is nondifferent from Śaṁkara's indeterminable and formless Being. But Śaṁkara made the mistake of assuming that Energy or Creativity cannot belong to the essential structure of Being. From the ultimate standpoint of Being, energy, change, evolution, etc. must be unreal. The main reason behind this line of thinking that Śaṁkara pursued is that he could not think of energy or creativity as anything other than a quality or attribute of some substance. Since substance-quality is merely a subjective mode of human apprehension, Śaṁkara concluded that Being must be void of energy (*Śaktimukta*).

But in ultimate analysis, what is true of Being is true of Energy also. Energy, power, or creativity (*Śakti*) is not a mere category of the intellect. Nor is it a mere quality or attribute of Being. It is the essential structure of Being. Better still, it is nondifferent from Being. Being is Energy, Energy is Being. Energy or Creativity is no less indeterminable and indescribable than Being. This perfect equation: Being = Energy (*Sat* = *Śakti*), is the most fundamental ontological insight of integral nondualism (*pūrṇa advaita*). "Just as we cannot separate fire from the power of fire, so also we cannot separate Energy from Being."[7] Transcending all names and forms, outsoaring all logical notions and philosophical categories, Being-Energy is boundless, unfettered, creative freedom.

It follows from the above that the perpetually changing cosmic manifold flowing from Being-Energy—the expanding universe of space, time, and evolution—is no less real than the indeterminable Being, the creative ground of the universe. Changing, evolving, self-actualizing individuals are no less real than the universal creative energy perpetually engaged in projecting planets and satellites, stars and galaxies.

An unwarrantable metaphysical assumption of ancient philosophy was that the permanent alone is real. A contemporary reaction to this ancient metaphysical belief is the equally untenable assumption that change or evolution alone is real. In the view of integral philosophy, change and permanence, time and eternity, evolution and involution are equally real dimensions of the same Being-Energy (*Sat-Śakti*).

The Supermind as Dichotomy-Dissolving Consciousness

Being-Energy is the dynamic source of all the dualities of existence and dichotomies of thought. Matter and mind, body and soul, nature and spirit, world and God, existence and essence, fact and value, Being-in-itself and Being-for-itself—these are all divergent modes of self-expression of the same cosmic energy which freely creates out of the immeasurable depths of its own Being. Nature is the creativity of Being in its unconscious mode of operation. Spirit is the same creativity in its conscious or superconscious mode of operation.

---

[7] Sri Aurobindo, *The Life Divine*, p. 314.

In the opinion of Jean-Paul Sartre, Nature is Being-in-itself, whereas man as conscious existence is Being-for-itself.[8] This is no other than an existentialist version of the age-old distinction between Nature and Spirit. In man's free creation of his culture and civilization, it is the creativity of Nature herself which acquires new dimensions. Ideas, essences, laws, principles, gods and goddesses are new values that emerge at the human level resulting from the interaction between man's creative consciousness and the world around him. They are not entirely subjective, or mere figments of the imagination. Nor are they things-in-themselves existing apart from the creative energy of human consciousness. They are subject-object determinations characteristic of the human world, or of the universe-as-apprehended-by-man.

Matter and mind are different grades of manifestation of the same creative energy (*Prakṛti, Śakti*).[9] When physico-chemical forces attain to a suitable degree of complexity of structure and function giving rise to the human organism and its nervous system with the brain, the newly emergent power of mind as reflective consciousness evolves as its distinctive characteristic. It is not a separate metaphysical principle, but a functional difference that distinguishes the human type of existence or energy-configuration.

At the heart of human consciousness is also to be detected another remarkable ability—the ability to distinguish between truth and falsehood, beauty and ugliness, good and evil, God and devil. This ability for spiritual discernment, accompanied by the spirit of love and devotion directed to intrinsic values, is the essence of the human soul. But the soul, or what Sri Aurobindo calls the psychic being, is not a separate and discontinuous metaphysical principle. It represents a qualitative and functional difference that imparts unique value and impor-

---

[8] Jean-Paul Startre, *Being and Nothingness* (New York: Philosophical Library, 1956), pp. LXVII, 73-105. Also his *Existential Psycho-Analysis* (New York: Philosophical Library, 1953), p. 3.

[9] Sri Aurobindo, *The Life Divine*, p. 83.

tance to the human type of existence.

It follows that what originally appeared as the dualities of existence, such as matter and mind, body and soul, are revealed, in ultimate analysis, as different grades of manifestation of the same creative energy of evolution. The distinctions involved here are certainly not unreal, false, or illusory. They are very real and significant. But to be sure, they do not constitute any division, separation, or fissure in the heart of Being. They do not amount to any ontological discontinuity shattering the unity of Being. They truthfully represent qualitative and functional differences unfolding in the course of evolution to enrich life and to make the world so exciting and fascinating.

Be it noted that the aforesaid interpretation of the dualities of existence in terms of the evolutionary energy of Being is slightly different from that of Sri Aurobindo. Responsibility for this interpretation belongs to none other than the present writer. But it is believed that the above interpretation is a logical sequel to the basic position of integral nondualism. The essence of the latter consists in combining the undivided unity of Being-Energy with the acceptance of the value and reality of the world of multiplicity.

The Metaphysics of the Supermind

The supermind is not only the highest kind of knowledge available to man. In the writings of Sri Aurobindo, it also has metaphysical, mystical, and cosmological implications.

Sri Aurobindo maintains that the supermind is "the comprehensive truth-consciousness" of Being in its highest manifestation, namely, the Absolute Spirit or Supreme Person (*Iśwara*). Traditional Vedānta lays stress upon the triune essence of the Supreme Spirit such as existence *(Sat)*, consciousness *(Cit)*, and bliss *(Ānanda)* —*Saccidānanda*. The supermind as the vast truth-consciousness is the fourth intrinsic characteristic of the Supreme.[10] It is

---
[10] Ibid., pp. 246, 291.

not only the fourth (*tūrīya*) from above, but also the fourth from below. It is above the cosmic triplicity of matter, life, and mind. It is the creative medium of manifestation of the infinite and eternal Spirit into the space-time world of matter, life, and mind. It is also the uplifting medium through which man can rise to attain comprehensive realization of the Supreme in its integral fullness, i.e. as the undivided unity of eternal perfection and perpetual evolution.

In medieval interpretations of the Vedānta, the supermind was ignored in metaphysical construction as well as in yogic discipline. As a result, the organic and essential relationship between the infinite, eternal, indeterminable Spirit on the one hand and the space-time world of variation and evolution on the other was not adequately grasped. This gave rise to varying degrees of world-and-life-negating tendencies and the consequent exaltation of asceticism, monasticism, and mystical indifference to social, economic, scientific, and political values of existence.

Realization of the Supreme on the supramental level of consciousness corrects this onesidedness and inadequacy, and restores the balance of outlook. It throws light upon the meaning of the world-process and of human evolution as the unceasing medium of manifestation of endless possibilities inherent in the Infinite Spirit.

At this point a critical inquiry might not be out of place. Is the Supreme Being or Infinite Spirit a substantive reality endowed with the essential attributes of consciousness, bliss, and supramental knowledge, and existing independently of, and prior to, the world process? If so, how do you know? What empirical or experiential evidence is there? Is not the notion of one infinite spiritual substance or all-knowing, all-blissful Existent a merely intellectual construction (*buddhinirmāṇa*) transcending all authentic mystic realization whether in the mode of *samādhi, nirvāṇa* or cosmic consciousness? Is it not an unverifiable speculative hypothesis subject to challenge by other rival hypotheses which are nonetheless sympathetic to mystic experience?

The idea of Being as one Supreme Spiritual Substance is definitely inconsistent with the affirmation of Being as indeterminable. In this respect Buddha's equation of indeterminable Being with Nonbeing or Emptiness is logically most consistent. The metaphysical notion of Being as one all-inclusive substantive Spirit militates against the antimetaphysical mood of contemporary philosophy as well as radical theology. Being as the ground of all beings can hardly be equated with any specific type of Being. Being as the all-encompassing medium of all existents can hardly itself be an existent.

Limitations of space would not permit us to go into any further elaboration of the above comments. Suffice it to say here that in the view of the present writer Existence-Consciousness-Bliss-Supermind (*Saccidānanda-Vijñāna*) is an excellent phenomenological description of man's most integral experience of Being-Energy, just as the "boundless blue sky" is a good phenomenological description of our perceptual experience of cloudless outer space. But it does not denote any infinite spiritual substance.

There can be no reasonable objection to the affirmation of the supermind as man's most profound spiritual potential. It is the cognition of Being in its integral fullness born of the total integration of human personality.

The Supermind and Mystical Cosmology

According to Sri Aurobindo the material world (*bhuḥ, anna*) in which we live is not the only projection of the Supreme Spirit. There are broadly speaking, six other complete planes of existence or types of world as divergent manifestations of the Supreme. These are: the vital (*bhuvaḥ, prāṇa*), the mental (*swaḥ*), the supramental (*Mahas*), the psychic (*jana, ānanda*), the dynamic spiritual (*tapas, cit*), and the ontological (*satya*).[11]

---

[11] Ibid., pp. 235-37. See also Sri Aurobindo, *On the Veda* (Pondicherry: Sri Aurobindo Ashram, 1964), pp. 47-48.

In the material world (*bhuḥ*) in which we live, matter is the matrix of all existence and the nurse of all becoming. But other structural principles of Being such as life, mind, supermind, psyche, spiritual energy, and pure being are also present in matter from the very beginning in a state of involution. That is why in the course of evolution the other constituents of Being can become manifest and overtly operative as suitable empircial conditions present themselves.

Similarly, there are vital, mental, supramental, and other higher planes of existence-consciousness. In each of these planes the metaphysical principle corresponding to its name is predominantly active as both the foundation and the regulating agency. For instance, in the supramental world, the supermind is the foundation and overtly operative principle. Physical, vital, mental and other energies are arranged and organized there in the light of the integral consciousness of the supermind.

Let us frankly admit that from the empirical standpoint the aforesaid theory of higher spirit-worlds is no more than a hypothesis which can hardly be proved conclusively. It is no doubt a hypothesis which can beautifully explain some yogic-mystical or occult experiences. But the same experiences are probably capable of being explained in other ways in terms of the known laws of nature without postulating any hierarchy of supraphysical spirit-worlds.

However, at the present state of our incomplete scientific knowledge it would certainly be wise to keep an unbiased and open mind, without slamming the door upon any possibility, however occult or mysterious. The doctrine of a hierarchy of spirit-worlds opens limitless new vistas of thought. They constitute fascinating new fields of research to which parapsychology and transpersonal psychology may direct their careful investigation. But a cautious approach would at this time posit them as emerging levels of consciousness man is capable of attaining on the fulfillment of certain conditions. There is no warrant for hypostatizing such emerging levels of consciousness as eternally pre-existent supernatural planes sustained by a supernatural Deity.

The Supermind as an Evolutionary Principle

In the view of integral philosophy, the supermind is not only a profound spiritual potential of man, but also a dynamic potential of the evolutionary impetus of Nature.

Rationalism holds that reason is the highest glory of man. But the last two great world wars and the increasing complication of international power politics ever since have shattered our rationalistic optimism. Existentialism is trying its best to come to terms with the absurd or irrational side of man. Psychoanalysis has disclosed the presence of the death instinct in man in all its naked ugliness.

But recent developments in depth psychology and parapsychology have revealed that in the depths of the human psyche dwell side by side unsuspected powers of light—those of profound intuitive wisdom, extrasensory perception and egoless love—as well as the terrible powers of darkness and destruction. The rise of transpersonal psychology in our present day amounts to the discovery of a new frontier in our psychological knowledge. It acknowledges the importance of authentic mystic experiences and other value-experiences inspiring self-actualizing persons the world over. It is realized that without an understanding of what Abraham Maslow has called "peak experiences,"[12] including the esthetic, the romantic, the ethico-religious, and the mystical, there is no possibility of gaining an adequate insight into the mystery of the human psyche in its creative richness. Such experiences transcend the subject-object dichotomy. They are not only mind-expanding, mind-changing, and creative, but also revelatory of new depths and dimensions of Being.

Empiricism affirms the Being of the world of sense experience in which we live. Rationalism affirms the Being

---

[12] Abraham Maslow, *Religions, Values and Peak Experiences* (Columbus: Ohio State University Press, 1964), pp. XI-XVI.

of the realm of Ideas which cast light upon the sensible world. Traditional mysticism affirms the ultimate reality of Being as the nameless, formless mystery, as the self-sufficient eternal. The significance of the supermind as integral consciousness is, as we have seen, that both the unchanging eternal and the evolutionary flux of time are equally real dimensions of the same integral Being. Thus the empirico-rational approach is harmoniously fused with the mystical orientation in the comprehensive outlook of integral philosophy.

In the view of integral philosophy, we stand today on the threshold of a new breakthrough in terrestrial evolution. Just as the fragmentary self-consciousness of the human mind one day evolved out of the matrix of animal consciousness, so the integral consciousness of the supermind looms large in the offing as the next emergent value in store for human evolution.

Confronted with the global problems of overpopulation, environmental pollution, possible atomic annihilation, the suicidal power play of international politics, etc., the collective consciousness of mankind is stirred to the depths. A process of anguished soul-searching and total churning of the human psyche is on. Out of this churning of the collective unconscious is likely to emerge a new planetary consciousness, the supermind, as a dynamic force in world affairs.

The integral consciousness of the supermind consists in the apprehension of diversity-in-unity sustained by the creative energy of nondual Being. So the new supramental age is likely to witness the founding of world unity without any violent regimentation of life and thought. It may herald the dawn of world peace without suppression of individual freedom and national self-determination.

The supermind, the unifying and transforming power of integral consciousness, is essential for the perfect integration of man's total being. As the creative energy of unitive consciousness, it is also essential for the unification of the human race.

Chapter 18

MODERN SCIENCE AND INTEGRAL PHILOSOPHY

It was stated in the first chapter that integral philosophy is a comprehensive world view inspired by integral experience of Being in its manifold richness of content. It was further stated that the rational foundation for the integral world view is provided by a self-coherent coordination of all sources of knowledge. First, there is the need for coordination and integration of such various phases of personal experience as perception, dream, sleep and transcendental consciousness (jāgrat, swapna, suśupti and samādhi or tūrīya). Secondly, there is the need for coordination and harmonization of such various disciplines of knowledge as science, art, morality, religion and mysticism.

The purpose of this chapter is to discuss briefly the profound philosophical significance of revolutionary discoveries in modern science. It will be seen that the radically changed world view of contemporary scientific thinking is not only perfectly compatible with, but also complementary to, the world view of man's authentic spiritual traditions both eastern and western.

Integral philosophy brings together in a harmonius fusion the seemingly conflicting world views of science and spirituality. It holds that whereas science discloses the relational structure of the infinitely differentiated universe, spirituality provides a glimpse of the mystery of Being, the ultimate ground of the same universe, the nontemporal depth dimension of the cosmic whole.

The Systems View of Modern Science

Recent revolutionary changes in various sciences have given rise to a radically new world view designated the Systems View.[1] It involves the rejection of the atomistic and mechanistic outlook as well as the absolute objectivism and value-neutralism of older days.

The old theory of atoms as indivisible particles of matter with definite locations in space succumbs to the modern scientific revolution and yields place to the notion of atom as an organized structure or system of electrons, protons and neutrons. These latter again are found to be structures of the cosmic flow of energy without rigidly fixed positions in space and inseparably mingling with other forces in a unified field of energy (Einstein). Every atom as a system of energy reveals unique characteristics which can hardly be reduced to the properties of its components.[2]

The old theory of absolutely objective knowledge resulting from the detached and value-free observation of the scientist's mind is also exploded. It is now realized that all knowledge, contemplation or observation is a creative process, an active transaction between knower and known. It invariably involves a two-way traffic, a flow of energy between subject and object. In the scientist's act of knowing, involving interest and attention in a definite direction, there is always a sense of purpose and value motivating the knower. Both knower and known get a little changed through the knowing process. Max Planck's quantum mechanics and Heisenberg's doctrine of uncertainty have demonstrated this truth with abundant clarity.

When the systems view of contemporary science is applied in the domain of psychology, some profound spiritual truths intuitively known to ancient sages become perfectly clear. The systems view beholds the universe as a hier-

---

[1] Ervin Laszlo, The *Systems View of the World* (New York: George Braille, 1972).
[2] Ibid., p. 8.

archical structure of system within system . . . represent-
able as ever-expanding concentric circles. The human individual as a system is thus a microcosmic representation
of the macrocosmic whole. If the macrocosmic reality is
the infinite self-representative system, then the individual
is an image, a reproduction, infinitely self-representing and
self-reflective part of the whole. The individual self is
thus revealed in a profound sense as one with the infinite
whole. Josiah Royce made this point very clear on the
basis of the modern mathematics' positive conception of
the infinite as a self-representative system (Kette).[3]

The Hierarchy of Levels of Consciousness

Let us now turn to the application of the systems view
in the domain of spiritual growth. When a person with-
draws his attention from the outside world[4] and turns the
searchlight upon his own inner being, an internal process
of transformation is immediately set in motion. The inter-
actional flow of energy is shifted from the horizontal relationship between organism and environment to the vert-
ical relationship between the life energy (prāṇa) getting
mobilized at the base of the spinal cord (mulādhāra,
the center of physical consciousness) and the thought
energy intensifying at the top of the brain (sahasrāra, the
center of cosmic consciousness). This eventually leads to
the full flowering of man's potential for self-realization as
an integral part of the cosmic whole.

The cosmic vision of truth is not a matter of otiose contemplation. It involves radical transformation of personality. It culminates in the birth of a new self, in the emergence of a cosmically oriented individual, capable of re-
creating his whole pattern of life and action into an image
of his inner vision of truth, beauty and love.

Integral self-realization implies integrated awareness of

---

[3] Josiah Royce, *The World and the Individual,* First Series. London:
The Macmillan Co., 1927. Pp. 507-519.

[4] This is known in yogic terminology as pratyāhāra, followed by
dhāranā, concentration followed by dhyāma, meditation.

one's total being as a hierarchically arranged structure of systems, physical, biological, mental and spiritual, reflecting the hierarchical structure of the evolutionary process.

The investigator in the domain of consciousness—yogi, meditator, mystic, spiritual seeker, gnostic, poet-seer—starts with his body-consciousness as the firm foundation for the superstructure of his evolving spiritual life. He cannot afford to allow his imagination to float in the clouds. He cannot afford to allow his random reverie to detach him from his body and to plunge him in aimless drifting. His first order of business is to get firmly rooted in physical consciousness. To this end a carefully cultivated, strong nervous system is indispensable.

With his feet firmly planted on the ground, the spiritual investigator is ready to undertake the steep mountain climbing of meditation, exploring higher and higher levels of consciousness. When in the course of consciousness-probing his social awareness is expanded, he joyfully experiences himself as a unique system of creative energy forming an integral part of the larger social organism to which he belongs. This entails a heightening of his sense of responsibility coupled with an intense joy of unique creativity. The ensuing experience is a curious blend of rights and duties, of privilege and self-privation, of self-expansion and social obligation.

At a later stage the meditator experiences his own social system as an integral part of higher and higher human organizations differentiated within the one international human family. With the gradual expansion of his consciousness he experiences emotional identification with ever broadening systems of kinship. Thus is brought about an exquisite blossoming of his altruistic and humanistic love opening its petals of rich perfume to embrace the whole of humanity. To use yogic terminology, this joyous and loving self-expansion takes place on the opening of the heart-center (hridpadma, anāhata). He experiences what Martin Buber calls the joy of authentic I-Thou relationship between himself and his ever-widening circle of fellow beings. His ecstacy of love spontaneously flows from his ontological insight into the organic interrelatedness of all human beings in the dynamic unity of man's evolution on earth.

To those with a religious bent of mind, the opening of the heart center produces the indescribable joy of union with the divine spirit of love, the lord of beauty and harmony from whom the music of cosmic rhythm continuously flows. The yogi hears the enchanting celestial music of Krishna's magic flute—the music that ravishes his heart and enthralls his whole being.

At a still higher level of consciousness the pilgrim of the infinite perceives the whole of humanity as an integral part of the global environment blending into the immeasurable vastness of the inter-galactic system of the expanding universe. He can no more separate the evolving humanity marching on the road of evolution from the limitless expanse of cosmic nature. He experiences the cosmic environment as part of his own being. He experiences humanity as a whole as an integral part of the cosmic landscape. A mystic feeling of awe and reverence, a deep sense of all-pervasive sacredness, a thrilling upsurge of adoration and love, wells up from the depths of his being and reaches out to embrace the totality of existence. The cosmic whole stands revealed in all its mystic grandeur as the unfathomable unity of all systems, as the all-encompassing medium of all organic structures.

This cosmic vision of the existence-whole is unfolded on the opening of what yoga psychology calls the command center (ājñā cakra, the center of commanding wisdom).[5] The panoramic view of the boundless expanse of existence enraptures him to every fibre of his being. At this center a dynamic integration of knowledge and will occurs. Triumphantly achieved is perfect control of the motor apparatus as well as the sensory apparatus of the psychophysical system. Knowledge is no longer passive under-

---

[5] C.W. Leadbeater, *The Chakras*, 7th Ed. (Adyar, Madras: The Theosophical Publishing House, 1966), p. 10-15.

standing divorced from the capacity for self-actualization. Knowledge now becomes self-effectuating Real-Idea. It turns into cosmically oriented master wisdom capable of sovereign self-expression.

Having attained self-mastery the yogi now experiences within himself Śiva's dance of cosmic rhythm. Śiva dances with life and death, with creation and destruction in his two hands. He dances with love and redemption, with evolution and involution in his two hands. With one of his dancing feet he tramples upon the demon of darkness. With another he brings to full flowering the seeds of perfection dormant in all being. His movement is a spontaneous outflow of creative joy. His will is effortless and desireless self-expression. The moment he says, "Let there be light", lo and behold, the light is everywhere in all its pure effulgence.

Beyond the cosmic expanse (Nāda) is the supra-cosmic transcendence. It is the nontemporal depth dimension of the universe of Being as the cosmic reality. It is the abode of that ultimate mystery which beggars all description and shines as "deep dazzling darkness." It is the mystery of Being, the ultimate ground of the cosmic manifold and the all-embracing Self of all selves. Meister Eckhart calls it the "absolute nudity of Being." Buddha calls it Emptiness (Śūnyatā). Śamkara calls it the formless featureless Being (Nirguṇa Brahman). Lao-tze calls it the nameless Tao. In the Zohar, the Jewish form of theosophy, the infinite is known as the En-Sof, the hidden God, the innermost Being of Divinity.[6]

In modern times Martin Heidegger characterizes Being as transcendence as such and therefore nothingness. Being as the ground of all beings is Being-itself, which as the destiny of thought remains concealed and mysterious.[7] But whereas Heidegger thinks Being is the mysterious destiny of thought, the sages of the East maintain that the great

---

[6] Gershom G. Scholem, *Major Trends in Jewish Mysticism* (New York: Schocken Books, 1967), p. 207-8.

[7] William Barrett & H. Aiken (ed.). *Philosophy in the Twentieth Century*, Vol. 3 (New York: Random House, 1962), p. 281-87.

Silence which transcends all conceptual understanding is still capable of being luminously experienced in the depth of silence of one's own being. The transcendent is experientially immanent in man's transcendental consciousness (tūrīya).

Sri Aurobindo, the great sage of renascent India, speaks of the "luminous uttermost Superconscience." It is that fathomless Silence from the depths of which emerge determinate systems without number but which illimitably transcends all systems and planes of existence and eternally shines as creative freedom. Man as a dynamic center of Being is a luminous spark of that freedom.

The fearless pilgrim of Being who is determined not to stop short of the highest peak catches a glimpse of Being in all its majestic grandeur when the crown center is opened. This is known in Yoga as the sahasrāra, the thousand petalled lotus, the celesial meeting point of the finite and the infinite, of man and God.

At the thrilling touch of the Divine, the individual's spiritual potential blossoms now to the full. The ground-energy of his existence (Śakti) is blissfully united with the crowning glory of consciousness (Śiva). Profusely flowing from the superconscious union is the nectar of immortality (amrita), the ambrosia of time-transcending joy flooding the entire personality. All bonds of ignorance are broken, all doubts are dissolved, all shadows of fear disappear, and all impurities melt away.

Under the overwhelming impact of the transcendent Being-cognition it first appears that the liberated person's individuality is liquidated. He feels like a river merging in the ocean, or like a doll of salt melting in the water, or like a moth reduced to nothingness in the cosmic flame of divine love. But as the experience undergoes slow maturation, the mystic is reborn on the lotus of radiant love as a unique focus of the infinite. As I have pointed out elsewhere,[8] it is the erstwhile egocentric individuality

---

[8] Haridas Chaudhuri, *Integral Yoga* (Wheaton: Theosophical Publishing House, a Quest Book), 1974, p. 107. See also the author's *Sri Aurobindo: Prophet of Life Divine*.

which gets dissolved in the vastness of cosmic consciousness. Out of the ruins of the ego-self emerges the authentic transpersonal Self as a dynamic component of the cosmic reality.

Integral Knowledge

This is when man's search for truth reaches the multisplendored glory of total self-realization. Transcendental consciousness ripens into integral knowledge (pūrṇa jñāna).

How does integral knowledge differ from transcendental consciousness?

Transcendental consciousness is ecstatic union with pure transcendence, with the timeless dimension of Being. Integral knowledge is the total awareness of Being as the indivisible unity of eternity and time, of transcendence and evolution, of the encompassing emptiness and the cosmic process. It is the apprehension of Being as nondifferent from cosmic energy (Brahma-Śakti) of which silence and creativity are inseparable aspects. It is the cognition of the cosmic whole as the space-time continuum in which evolution builds hierarchies of emerging spheres. It is the realization of the Self as the consciousness-continuum in which inner growth unfolds ever-widening vistas of thought and towering heights of vision. The dichotomies of the unreal and the real as well as of the natural and the supernatural are revealed as projections of meaningful ignorance (māyā).

Integral knowledge represents complete integration of the departmental, cosmic and transcendental dimensions of consciousness. It is a harmonious fusion of the unconscious, conscious and superconscious aspects of personality. The secret of this harmony or integration is to be found in the fact that integral knowledge is the mature fruit of the integrated functioning of all the energy centers of the organism. A word of explanation might be in order here.

In integral knowledge the mystic vision is not divorced

from the body awareness. Nor does the mystic get up-rooted from his existential roots in the world. Nor is the empirical self rejected either as an evil or as an illusion. On the contrary, all the levels of personality are unified into a dynamic harmony oriented to the freely chosen goal of life. All the energy centers of the body function in unison.

Integration of the Energy Centers

The root center (mulādhāra) which preserves its communion with the crown center keeps the individual firmly planted on the ground and prevents his speculative immersion in an ivory tower or his ethereal flight into the cloud-cuckoo land of subjective fancy. It plays a part in integral knowledge by strengthening the yogi's self-image as a child of the evolving earth-energy.

The libido center (swādhisthāna) plays a part in integral knowledge by preventing premature suppression or ascetic annihilation of instinctual drives. It reveals their *raison d'etre,* allows their reasonable fulfillment in an organized scheme of living, and then in due time effectuates their transformation into subtle and luminous psychic energy (ojas). As a result, the libido center continues to function as a source of radiant health, boundless vitality and optimum longevity.

The power center (manipura) does not become a deserted ghost house rejected by higher consciousness. It also plays a vital role in integral knowledge as a source of unsuspected abilities for establishing the glory of truth and love in the world.

The love center (anāhata) blossoming at the caressing stroke of Being-energy fills the heart with the music of harmony with Being. Flowing from that music is the joyful spirit of self-giving for the good of all or for the sake of cosmic welfare. Love transforms the joy of being into the joy of giving, the delight of self-existence into the delight of sharing self-expression.

The throat center (viśuddha) illumined with knowledge and inspired with love uses the spoken word as an effective tool of communication of the truth of things as they are in their suchness, i.e. in respect of their unique and distinctive features.

The wisdom center (ajña) shines with the light of cosmic consciousness and reveals the universe in its unified wholeness of being. But in doing so it does not blot out the infinite richness of multicolored variations on the cosmic theme. It embraces infinite multiplicity in a flash of intuition and the infinite stream of time in an eternal now.

The crown center (sahasrāra) functioning in perfect unison with all the lower centers provides glorious insight into the nontemporal and indefinable depth dimension of existence. But the integral perspective does not allow this transcendental insight to be fragmented from the holistic and the differentiated aspects of the universe. On the contrary, functioning in perfect unison with all the lower centers, it transforms the whole of life into a symphony, into a sacred poem of divine delight. It serves as the mainspring of inspiration to integral man's active participation in the cosmic drama of the mind's adventures in the realm of matter.

Thus we see that integral philosophy unifies in its world-view the vision of pure transcendence beyond all systems and the evolutionary process of building system beyond system without end in the space-time continuum. The total truth is always the unity of opposites. In the ultimate context the integral truth is the unity of systems and no-system. It is thus the meeting ground of science and mysticism.

The Integral View and Systems View

We have seen how the integral view is in harmony with the systems view in regard to the relational structure of the universe. The difference lies in the fact that the integral view also affirms the nonrelational depth dimension of the universe. A clarification of the reasons for this difference is necessary before bringing this chapter to a close.

There are two essential respects in which the difference can be clearly recognized.

In the first place, it should be noted that every system is essentially a product of the creative energy of consciousness, of systematic thinking. But consciousness or thought itself is not to be completely equated with any definite system or objective structure. Consciousness is pure formless subjectivity. It is Kant's transcendental subject, not to be confused with the empirical subject or ego-self. It is the Mind as transcendental act, as Gentile would like to put it. It is *thought-thinking* as distinguished from *thought thought,* or *reflection reflecting* as distinguished from *reflection reflected.* It is indeterminable unobjectifiable transcendental consciousness, the Puruṣa of Sāṅkhya philosophy, the Ātman of Vedānta, and the Ālayavijñana of Mahāyāna Buddhism. That is why no religious creed or theological dogma, no scientific law or philosophical system, no ethical principle or political ideology can ever be said to deliver the last word of wisdom or absolute truth. Just as on the objective side the universe is an unending process of space-time continuum, so also on the subjective side pure consciousness is unceasing stream of self-transcendence.

Secondly, the cosmic whole in its fullness transcends all systems, however comprehensive or all-embracing. Reality divided by reason always leaves a remainder. After everything has been said about the universe, after the entire world has been transformed on the basis of scientific knowledge into a hierarchical structure of ever-widening systems, we are still invariably left with a profound sense of mystery. The unfathomable mystery which lies at the core of reality baffles both the analytical function of thought pointing to the infinitesimal as well as its synthetic function building higher and higher systems toward the infinite. This luminous experience of the impenetrable mystery is common to all the scientists, philosophers and mystics of the highest rank. The scientist calls it the mystery of Nature. The philosopher calls it the mystery of Being. The mystic calls it the mystery of the Spirit.

We feel that the essence of wisdom consists in recognizing the fullness of the ultimate mystery in its triune form. The supreme mystery of Being (Parabrahman) enfolds within itself the mystery of Nature (cosmic creative energy, Prakṛti, Śakti) as well as the mystery of the Spirit (the light of cosmic consciousness, Puruṣa, Śiva). This is the significance of the beautiful art work of the Lord Śiva with three faces (Trimurti). The face on the right side symbolizes the masculine aspect of Logos; the face on the left side symbolizes the feminine aspect of Eros, Love-energy; the face in the middle towering above the other two is the ground-unity of Being (Parabrahman).

Let us put it in another way. The universe in its essential structure has two inseparable dimensions: relational and nonrelational, spatio-temporal and nontemporal, rational and supra-rational. In respect of the first dimension the universe can be envisaged as a hierarchy of systems within systems within systems within . . . It is an intelligible scheme of relations and relata explicable in terms of laws, theories and working hypotheses.

In respect of the nontemporal depth dimension, the cosmic whole transcends all relations and distinctions. It transcends the dichotomies of whole and part, of subject and object, of system and reason. Every system of existence and energy is, in ultimate analysis, a product of interaction between the fullness of reality and rational consciousness, or between immediate existence and the mediating categories of thought. So it is absurd to equate any system, however comprehensive, with the entire universe or ultimate reality. The tendency to establish such an equation is inspired by the wishful thinking that ultimate reality is absolute thought or reason. Such wishful thinking leads to the dogmatic attitude of absolute certainty or ultimate finality. Dogmatism, ultimatism or finalism is the direct antithesis of genuine wisdom inspired by the insight into the inscrutable mystery of Being. The hallmark of wisdom is the spirit of humility.

The truth of the above remarks is illustrated in the absolutistic orientations of Hegel and Marx. Hegel develops the system of absolute idealism and believes that it represents the absolute truth or the essential structure of ultimate reality. He therefore concludes that the ultimate goal of evolution and history would be perfect embodiment of the truth of absolute idealism—the German State as the Absolute Spirit. Likewise Marx develops the system of dialectical materialism and believes that it represents the ultimate structure of reality as history. He therefore concludes that the ultimate goal of evolution and history would be perfect embodiment of *his* vision of human destiny—an international world order of communism. Both of these dogmatic ideologies are animated by the false equation of Being with a determinate thought system.

Whereas a theological, metaphysical, or political thought system is more speculative than empirical, a scientifically developed system of theories and laws is more empirical than speculative. Nonetheless, the latter also contains a speculative, conceptual, or theoretical component. A theory or law is essentially a conceptual structure postulated to explain certain experiential data. It is always subject to revision, modification, or rejection in the light of fresh factual discoveries.

Moreover, the so-called empirical data of immediate experience are never absolutely immediate. Absolute immediacy is a figment of imagination. The so-called facts of observation and experiment are, as F. H. Bradley rightly observes, our half-thought-out theories. They are invariably the outcome of thought's selective and differentiating function working upon the undifferentiated plenum of immediate experience. They spring from interaction between reality and the perceptive mind, between energy vibrations and the sensorium of the human brain. So it may be said that every perceived fact of existence (e.g. a happily singing red bird in a green tree) is a sense-modified, purposely selected, and subjectively interpreted item of one's experience-continuum.

To equate any differentiated group of perceptual data with the infinite fullness of existence is incompatible with the purposive selectivity of all human knowledge. The human mind is under the inescapable limitation of selecting and abstracting from the infinite fullness of existence in the interest of its survival or its creative freedom and personal fulfillment. This imparts to all our knowledge only a relative measure of validity. By its very nature our knowledge is bound always to fall short of the immeasurable vastness of the real.

The integral outlook therefore rejects dogmatism in all forms, whether scientific or metaphysical, religious or political. On the objective side it glimpses the mystery of Nature (Prakṛti) beyond the scientifically revealed rational structure of the world. On the subjective side it glimpses the mystery of formless consciousness or Spirit (Puruṣa) beyond the variegated levels and structures of the mind. Beyond both Nature and Spirit, beyond both the objective and the subjective, it envisions the supreme mystery of Being (Brahman) which is the ultimate ground of both.

Conclusion

We are now in a position to sum up the essence of integral philosophy in the form of one fundamental equation: The universe=Energy=Being (Jagat=Śakti=Śiva). The basic energy sustaining the cosmic flow is nondifferent from indeterminable Being or absolute Void, Vedāntic Brahman or Buddhist Śūnyatā which projects endless names and forms without the slightest impoverishment.

Science deals with the interrelations, causal connections, or acausal synchronicities between endless names and forms, events and processes, of the cosmic flow. By conceptualizing them in terms of interrelated systems or increasingly complex structures of energy, modern science brings them together into the organismic or systems view of the universe. It affirms the reality of consciousness as the systemic or gestalt property of the human organism. It establishes the finitude of man, the selectivity of all cognitive functions, and the consequent relativity of all human knowledge.

Whereas science perceives the oneness of all existence in terms of the unity of cosmic energy, mysticism perceives the oneness of all existence as the diversified expression of Being. Scientific investigation of Nature culminates in unitive knowledge of the unified energy-field. Mystic or yogic exploration of consciousness culminates in the flowering of cosmic truth-vision and transmutive love. The ontological insight born of integrated spiritual experience affirms the ultimate reality of nondual Being which is one with cosmic energy. Such insight provides the key to the integration of all human knowledge on the one hand, and to the unification of all human life in a global society on the other.

Mahatma Gandhi demonstrated not long ago the transmutive power of unitive consciousness by bringing together the divergent races, religions, and parties of the Indian subcontinent in their combined struggle for freedom. He did it on the national level. With the evolutionary expansion of the same kind of unitive truth-vision it may not be impossible for mankind to achieve in the near future effective liberation from violence and greed, and from division and discord, with spiritual weapons of understanding and love.

Unitive truth-vision implies the apprehension of the many as a spontaneous outpouring of the creative One. It also implies the apprehension of the One as the creative unity of the many. At the supramental level, it implies a glimpse of the mystery of nondual Being in which all unifying principles are grounded.

For instance, unitive truth-vision reveals the divergent world religions as essentially many-in-one, because the Gods of various religions are different historical perspectives of the same Being as revealed to man's religious consciousness. The same is true of ethics, politics and other areas of human experience. All ethical principles are essentially many-in-one, because they are applications in life's changing circumstances of the one basic law of human evolution, to wit, the law of subservience to creative growth. All political ideologies also are essentially many-in-one, because they are formulations, in different socio-cultural and economico-political conditions, of the same basic human aspiration for collective and unified self-actualization on earth.

Likewise, the different seemingly conflicting disciplines of knowledge such as science, art, morality and religion are essentially many-in-one, because they reveal different facets of the same ultimate Being. Corresponding to the different facets of Being, there are different dimensions of human experience and knowledge. For instance, science represents the harmony of facts and ideas corresponding to the rational structure of the universe. Art represents the harmony of sensations and feelings corresponding to the esthetic continuum of the universe. Morality represents the harmony of impulses and desires corresponding to the ethical order and balance of the universe. Religion represents the harmony of individuals and the cosmic reality corresponding to the nontemporal ground-aspect of the universe.

The more this cosmic truth-vision becomes a dynamic factor in our consciousness, the more we can join forces with our fellow beings regardless of race, religion, and nationality, in building one harmonious structure of peace, justice, and love on earth.

This is the meaning of what Sri Aurobindo calls material immortality as the ultimate goal of human evolution.

INDEX

OTHER QUEST BOOK TITLES